The publishers wish to thank
Gibson Guitar Corp.

for the use of the Gibson Montana
CL40 Artist Acoustic Guitar featured on the cover

along with
Neumann USA

for the use of the U-87 microphone
also featured on the cover.

Cover Photography by
Susana Millman
Coverage Photography
San Francisco, CA

Contents

Chapter Four   33

Miking Instruments

WITHDRAWN
Professional
MICROPHONE TECHNIQUES

By:

David Miles Huber

and

Philip Williams

236 Georgia Street • Suite 100 • Vallejo • CA 94590

artistpro.com
THE RECORDING INDUSTRY NETWORK

Library of Congress Catalog Card Number: 98-067693

Production Staff: Mike Lawson, Publisher
Bill Gibson, Editor/Layout/Illustrator; Linda Gough, Cover Designer

MixBooks is an imprint of artistpro.com, LLC
236 Georgia Street, Suite 100
Vallejo, CA 94590
707-554-1935

Also from MixBooks:

The AudioPro Home Recording Course, Volumes I, II, and III
Studio Business Book
Live Sound Reinforcement
The Art of Mixing: A Visual Guide to Recording, Engineering, and Production
The Home Studio Guide to Microphones
The Songwriter's Guide to Collaboration, Rev. and Exp. 2nd Ed.
I Hate the Man Who Runs This Bar!
Critical Listening and Auditory Perception
Professional Microphone Techniques
The Mixing Engineer's Handbook
Ruthless Self-Promotion in the Music Industry
How to Run a Recording Session, 2nd Ed.
Booking, Promoting and Marketing Your Music Career
Essentials of Music for Audio Professionals
Music Producers, 2nd Ed.
Music Publishing: The Real Road to Music Business Success, Rev. and Exp. 5th Ed.
Sound for Picture, 2nd Ed.
The Mastering Engineer's Handbook
The Professional Musician's Internet Guide
Professional Sound Reinforcement Techniques

Also from EMBooks:

Anatomy of a Home Studio
The Independent Working Musician
Making the Ultimate Demo, 2nd Ed.
Remix: The Electronic Music Explosion
Making Music with Your Computer, Rev. Ed.

Printed in Auburn Hills, MI
ISBN 0-872886-85-9

Chapter Five   85

Miking Vocals and Speech

Chapter Six   97

Stereo Miking Techniques

Chapter Seven   111

Outboard Stuff

Chapter Eight   125

The CD

Chapter 1 An Introduction to Microphones

So ya wanna know more about mic techniques? Where should you place them? How should they be used to get the best sound for a particular instrument and recording situation? Which kind get the most natural sound or that effect that you've always wanted? Well, sit back and read, then load the corresponding audio CD examples into your player and listen for yourself to a culmination of years of experience and dedication to the art of miking instruments in both professional and project studios.

What's this book all about?

It's about guidelines! By far the best way to use this book is to first study all the examples of instruments, miking styles and vocal techniques; then, try them for yourself in your own studio environment. Once you've put our techniques to the test and gained a practical working knowledge of mic placement, your job (should you choose to accept it) is to take technology to the next step by experimenting on your own to create your unique, personal style. Remember, recording is an art... you should always feel free to paint your own sound canvas.

Let's start down the road to understanding miking techniques with a few simple rules:

Rule #1

There are no rules, only guidelines.

Rule #2

Use the "Good Rule", whenever possible, which states: Good Source + Good Placement + Good Mic = Good Sound

This elusive, artistic maxim basically states that a music track will only be as good as the performer, the instrument, the mic placement and the mic. If all these factors are the best they can be, the track will be great! If any of them falter, the recording will suffer accordingly.

Rule #3

Don't try to "fix it in the mix."

Whenever possible, avoid the "Band-Aid" concept of fixing a problem later, during mixdown. Masking deficiencies by using EQ or other effects might help smooth over a problem, but it's a poor substitute for getting the right sound onto tape the first time. Trust us, getting it right on tape will help the mix go smoother and the project will sound much better.

In the final analysis, miking instruments in the studio or on stage is definitely an art, and the best rule of all is: **follow your common sense**. *Professional Microphone Techniques* offers a set of guidelines to help you understand the process of miking.

When you get right down to it, this book falls into four basic categories which are designed to give you:

1. A basic understanding of microphone technology

2. An understanding of the environment where the recording is to take place

3. An understanding of how to manipulate the relationship between the mic and room acoustics, as a function of miking distance

4. A set of concise simple guidelines to help determine which mics to use and where to place them for various alphabetically-ordered instruments

These are all extremely important and valuable tools for successfully miking an instrument or ensemble. Make no mistake about it, these insights come with time, practice and dedication. However, we've included several pointers to help you get started:

Since certain general principles apply to miking any instrument, it's generally a good idea to know what kind of sound is needed before you start setting up mics. Every instrument has a *sweet spot* where a microphone picks up the most natural or pleasing sound. This sweet spot can be found by listening carefully to the instrument as it's being played. The spot where the instrument sounds the way you want it to is probably is a pretty good place to put the mic.

This book is full of examples demonstrating various types of sweet spots for various types of instruments, styles and personal preferences (See Chapter 4). You'll find references to the included audio CD throughout the text. These let you actually hear the various techniques, miking styles and effects, first hand.

Now, we invite you to sit back, read, ponder, listen and then apply these techniques to your own music and/or music productions. Have fun and dive into the deep end!

David Miles Huber
Philip L. Williams

Chapter 2 Mic Types and Characteristics

Types and Characteristics

Beyond the obvious, there are a couple of things you should know about transducer design:

1. It's notoriously difficult to design a device that accurately converts acoustical energy to corresponding electrical voltages.

2. They're designed by human beings who started out with a subjective idea of how they wanted them to sound and how they wanted them to operate.

Because of these two factors, very few mics are physically or sonically alike, each having its own set of strengths, characteristics and quirks. Although the various mic types, specs and general characteristics have been explained in other books, we thought we'd give you a quick and concise 5 cent tour of the basic inner-workings of the professional microphone. We do this for one reason, and one reason alone: when one understands how a mic works and what characteristics it displays, the job of understanding which mic to choose for a particular application is easier.

How They Work

Not all mics are created equal; each one has it's own sonic characteristic that sets it apart from other mics. There are, however, factors that differentiate one mic from the next other than their basic operating types. The three mic types that can be found in professional and project recording studios are: dynamic, ribbon, and condenser. The following set of simple and short explanations are intended to give you an insight into how each of these work and, therefore, into their unique and characteristic sound.

The Dynamic Mic

Some of you may remember being shown in school how you can wrap a wire several times around an empty toilet paper tube, connecting the wires to a galvanometer—a meter that measures voltage and polarity. Then, by passing a magnetic stick in and out of the wire-wound tube, you could induce a measurable voltage into the wire that would vary in proportion to the magnet's direction and rate of movement. Well, folks, this process is called the electromagnetic theory of induction, and it demonstrates exactly how a dynamic mic works!

The diaphragm of a dynamic mic typically consists of Mylar plastic that has a finely wrapped coil of wire—called a voice coil—attached to its inner face. This coil is then precisely suspended within a strong magnetic field (Figure 2-1).

Whenever a sound-pressure wave hits the diaphragm (Figure 2-1, A), the attached voice coil (Figure 2-1, B) is displaced in proportion to

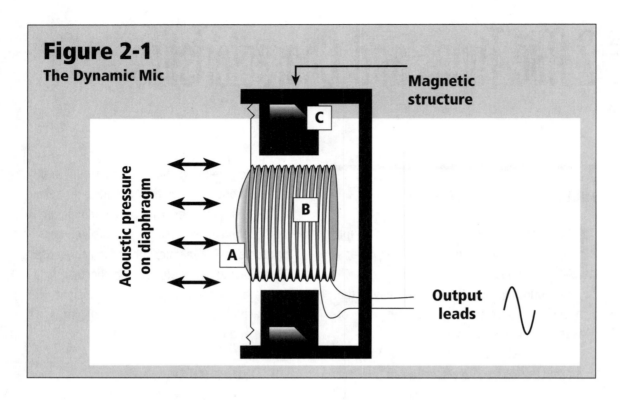

Figure 2-1
The Dynamic Mic

Magnetic structure

Acoustic pressure on diaphragm

C

B

A

Output leads

the amplitude and frequency of the wave, causing the coil to cut across the lines of magnetic flux supplied by the permanent magnet (Figure 2-1, C). Due to the electromagnetic theory of induction—which states that whenever a metal cuts across a magnetic field, a current will be induced into that metal—an output voltage of proportional magnitude and direction to the acoustic signal is generated across the voice coil leads. And voila, you have a dynamic mic!

Here's where it gets really interesting. Since the mass of the diaphragm and voice coil is actually quite large, compared to the energy that's contained in the acoustic signal, it takes time for the diaphragm to respond to a signal (i.e., to move). Due to this simple piece of physics, a dynamic mic responds to sharp transients much more poorly that any other professional mic type. In addition, once this mass gets

moving, it takes a bit of time for it to stop moving, even after the waveform is gone. It's much like trying to stop a person on a swing set: it take a few passes to come to rest.

Neither of these things are bad; they're just a large part of what gives the dynamic its characteristic gutsy, rugged and less-transparent sound (CD Track 2). This makes them perfect for lots of applications, such as certain types of vocals, amplified instruments and so forth. This rugged design also makes them perfect for rock and general knock-around applications.

The Ribbon Mic

The ribbon microphone, like the dynamic, operates on the same principle. However, instead of having a disc-like diaphragm, an extremely thin aluminum ribbon is suspended between two poles of a strong magnet. Quite simply, variations in sound pressure cause the ribbon to cut across the lines of magnetic flux, thereby inducing a voltage into the ribbon that's proportional in amplitude and frequency to the acoustic signal (Figure 2-2).

The ribbon mic is often called a velocity or pressure-gradient mic because the motion of the ribbon results from differences in pressure between its front and rear faces. Since certain ribbon designs are equally sensitive to sounds from both directions, sounds originating at the rear of the ribbon produce a voltage in the ribbon that's 180° out-of-phase with an equivalent signal at the front of the ribbon. This results in a bidirectional or figure eight pattern, unless the ribbon is mounted in a special housing that's designed to be cardioid, omni or switchable. Sound waves arriving 90° off axis— at the sides of the ribbon—produce an opposing pressure at both the front and rear of the ribbon, resulting in no output signal.

Ribbon mics—especially older models— are often fragile and easily damaged. This is due to the fact that the corrugated ribbon can be literally bent out-of-shape if it's hit with an excessive windblast. For this reason, older types (like the RCA 44 and 77 models) have large wind screens cages that protect them from day-to-day blasts.

It's extremely important to determine whether a ribbon microphone can be used in a system that has a phantom supply for powering condenser mics. Applying phantom power to many ribbon microphones—especially older types—can turn the ribbon into a big fuse, and blow it out! Some of the contemporary ribbon microphones, such as those made by Beyer, can

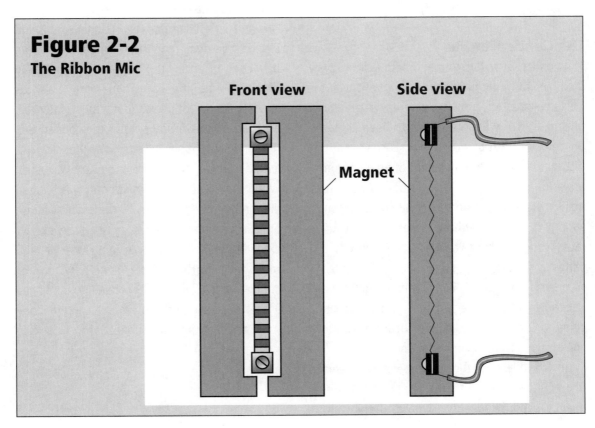

Figure 2-2
The Ribbon Mic

Front view   **Side view**

Magnet

be used with phantom power; however, check with the manufacturer before plugging any ribbon mic into any cable with phantom power. When in doubt, the best practice is simply not to use a ribbon mic in any system where the phantom supply can't be turned off.

As with any mic type, ribbon mics have their own unique sound. Some of the vintage ribbon microphones, like the squarish RCA Model 44s that are seen in old films, are quite smooth with a high frequency roll-off that results in a much sought-after mellow sound (CD Track 2).

The RCA Model 77 has a more extended frequency response than the Model 44, with the same silky smoothness. Contemporary cardioid ribbon mics, like those made by Beyer, have a good high-end response with the characteristic ribbon smoothness, but are rugged enough to use on stage (CD Tracks 2–3).

The Condenser Mic
The condenser mic is totally different from dynamic and ribbon microphones in that it works on an electrostatic principle whereby a very thin plastic or Mylar diaphragm, that's been coated on one side with gold or nickel, is spaced at a distance of about a thousandth of an inch from a stationary backplate. Once a polarizing voltage (in the form of a battery or 48 volt phantom supply) is applied to these plates, the two surfaces work together to create a capacitance that varies as the diaphragm is moved by the acoustic pressure of a sound wave. This change in capacitance is then detected by an electronic circuit and converted into an electrical signal that corresponds to the acoustic sound wave.

Typically, since the condenser's diaphragm is extremely light, both the transient and frequency response are very accurate, often result-

ing in a sound that's extremely clear and transparent (Figure 2–3, CD Track 2).

The Electret-Condenser Mic
Instead of requiring a voltage supply to power the condenser, an electret-condenser's capsule uses a permanent static electric charge—just like the static-cling that your clothes get in the wash—to make the capacitance work. Although these mics don't require a polarizing voltage, a battery or phantom voltage is needed to power a small preamp that follows the capsule. It's been said that the sensitivity of a well-designed electret capsule would drop by only 3 dB over a period of ten to a hundred years. So far, they're still going, and going, and going…

The Choice of Champions: Small vs. Large Diaphragm
A major difference between condensers is the size of their diaphragm. They range in size from a fraction of an inch to about 1 1/2 inches in diameter. This applies to dynamic as well as condenser microphones, though the greatest diameter range is found among the condensers. Ribbon microphones have ribbons that range in length from less than an inch to over two inches. When compared to large diaphragm mics, small diaphragm mics are typically the most accurate on axis, have better frequency response, exhibit extended high end and transient response, and reproduce more uniform directivity. Large-diaphragm mics, on the other hand, tend to have a full robust sound that's very pleasing in many vocal and instrumental applications.

Figure 2-3
Condenser Mics

"…a very thin plastic or Mylar diaphragm, that's been coated on one side with gold or nickel, is spaced at a distance of about a thousandth of an inch from a stationary backplate. Once a polarizing voltage (in the form of a battery or 48 volt phantom supply) is applied to these plates, the two surfaces work together to create a capacitance that varies as the diaphragm is moved by the acoustic pressure of a sound wave. This change in capacitance is then detected by an electronic circuit and converted into an electrical signal that corresponds to the acoustic sound wave."

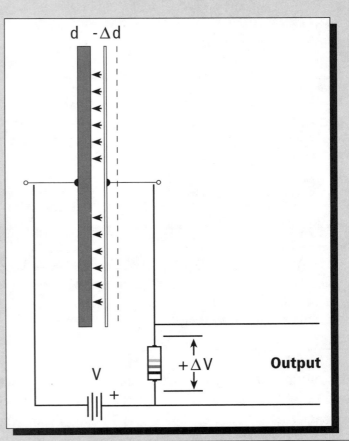

Frequency Response

Frequency response can definitely play a part in determining which mic you choose. Typically, dynamic mics have the most erratic frequency response of the pickup types with ribbons having a slightly smoother response and condensers demonstrating the flattest and most extended response curve.

Again, this doesn't mean dynamic mics are bad; some have a very flat response characteristic. However, even those that aren't the flattest can be fantastic for certain applications. For example, it's not uncommon for certain mics to have a pronounced midrange bump—as with the Shure SM 57, SM 58 and their newer Beta reincarnations. This tends to accentuate the mid-frequencies on vocals and amp-speaker pickups, giving them a pickup character that's often highly sought after. It's also common to come across a ribbon or condenser that has its own frequency characteristics, which change the sound (Figure 2-4).

Microphones don't always perform equally under all circumstances. Certain frequency curves can help hide or accentuate aspects of an instrument's character. Since it's impossible for any one design to represent the perfect microphone, the frequency response of each mic

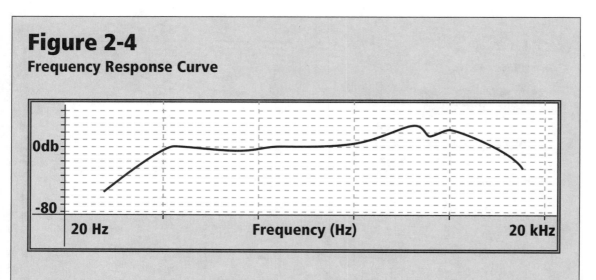

Figure 2-4
Frequency Response Curve

0db

-80

20 Hz   **Frequency (Hz)**   **20 kHz**

"…it's not uncommon for certain mics to have a pronounced midrange bump—as with the Shure SM 57, SM 58 and their newer Beta reincarnations. This tends to accentuate the mid-frequencies on vocals and amp-speaker pickups, giving them a pickup character that's often highly sought after.".

is acoustically tailored to function optimally within a specific application or range of applications.

Having said this, however, if you only want to buy a limited number of microphones, it's generally a good idea to start with a matched pair of natural sounding, wide range condenser mics. You should also have a good pair of dynamic mics, since these tend to work well on a wide range of instruments in most day-to-day miking applications.

On-axis Frequency Response

An on-axis frequency response curve represents the mic's response to sounds that originate from right in front of it. Generally, the flattest frequency response for a directional microphone is on-axis, with the response curve often varying greatly as the sound source is moved further off axis.

Off-axis Frequency Response

A directional mic's frequency-response curve, when measured off axis, can range from being flat to being "peaky" or erratic. When the latter occurs, signal coloration can be heard when the sound originates off axis (from the side of the mic). Often, the result is a change in the overall tone quality. Knowing the off-axis frequency response curve can be an effective tool for determining how sound reaching the mic off axis will be reproduced.

In music recording, a poor off-axis response can degrade the overall quality of a mix through frequency coloration and/or phase distortion of off-axis sounds. This is especially true when recording acoustic instruments, where the sound radiates from the entire instrument. Inadequate off-axis response in this situation can color the instrument's entire sound. In a public address or sound reinforcement application, a uniform off-axis frequency response (absent of severe peaks) is essential. An on-stage cardioid microphone that has a big off-axis peak in its operating range can receive too much energy at one frequency, causing feedback.

Low-Frequency Response Factors

A number of mics have a frequency response that's relatively flat from 20 Hz to 20 kHz. However, from a practical viewpoint, such a bandwidth response could cause unwanted signals to be picked up. For example, low-frequency rumble (high-level vibrations in the 3–25 Hz region) can be transmitted in a studio, hall or room—or along the surface of a large unsupported floor space. If such a condition exists, three possible solutions can be used:

1. Isolate the mic from the vibrating surface and floor stand by using a shock mount.
2. Choose a mic that has a restricted low-frequency response.
3. Restrict the low-frequency response by using a highpass (low-frequency cutoff) filter.

Proximity Effect

Many directional mics show an increase in their bass response as the signal source is brought closer to the microphone capsule. This phenomenon, known as proximity effect, starts to become noticeable when the source is brought to within one foot of the microphone and it increases as the distance decreases (CD Track 3).

To compensate for this, a low-frequency roll-off filter is often used to restore the bass response to a flat and natural balance. This filter is most often a selective switch that's located on the body of the mic. Certain mics, which are

designed to work at close distances, may be permanently rolled-off in the low-frequency range, using proximity effect to restore the response to its natural balance. One example of this is the clip mic, which uses a bass roll-off to compensate for the natural resonance of the human chest cavity.

Another, less well-known way to eliminate proximity effect, and the associated popping of the letters "p" and "b", when close-miking, is to replace the directional microphone with an omnidirectional mic.

On a positive note, vocalists and radio announcers have long appreciated proximity effect. In many cases it has become an important tool for giving a full, larger-than-life quality to some pretty thin sounding voices.

Polar Patterns

The polar pattern of a mic refers to a mic's level sensitivity and frequency response over a full 360° circle, relative to its on-axis readings. The on- and off-axis response of a microphone often is depicted as a polar response chart. This chart has a series of concentric circles—marked in angular degrees—which indicate the off-axis levels, relative to the pickup's reference on-axis level. The on-axis of the microphone is at 0°; completely off-axis for a cardioid mic is at 180° (Figure 2-5).

Omnidirectional

Omnidirectional (omni) mics pick up sound uniformly from all directions. This pattern has been much maligned by the industry, as it generally produces a very natural sound. It offers the least off-axis coloration of any pattern type and is an extremely good choice when close-miking, since it doesn't exhibit proximity effect. When distant-miking, this type of mic could be used to capture wanted reflections from all around the room.

While an omni mic is intended to pick up sounds equally from all directions, in reality it tends to become directional at high frequencies and doesn't pick up off-axis high frequencies as well. So, even though the mic isn't directional, per se, it should still be aimed at the intended sound source.

Cardioid

A cardioid mic gets its name from the fact that its polar response chart is heart shaped. This pattern is designed to fully pick up sound that originates from in front (on-axis at 0°) and to reduce the pickup levels at the sides (90° and 270°) by about 6 dB while rejecting sounds that originate from the rear (180° off-axis).

Cardioid mics suppress sound that origi-

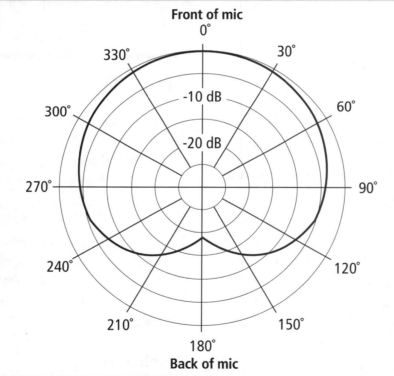

Figure 2-5
Microphone Polar Response Chart

"…a polar response chart …has a series of concentric circles—marked in angular degrees—which indicate the off-axis levels, relative to the pickup's reference on-axis level. The on-axis of the microphone is at 0°; completely off-axis for a cardioid mic is at 180°"

nates from the rear by 15–25 dB, thereby reducing leakage, noise, and excessive reverberation. They can be used at greater distances from a sound source and typically provide a sense of spatial location when used in a stereo configuration.

Supercardioid

A supercardioid mic is least sensitive at a point about 125° off axis. It has less sensitivity at the sides than a cardioid mic does (typically being down about 8–9 dB) and its sound rejection at the rear is down about 15 dB. This type of mic is used where side rejection is preferred while capturing some ambience through the small area of sensitivity directly off axis.

Hypercardioid

A hypercardioid mic is used when a maximum side rejection is desired, such as on a drum kit where the hi-hat needs to be isolated from the snare, or where two musicians are playing close together. Hypercardioid mics tend to reject reverberation and background noises more than the other mic types. While a hypercardioid mic has the greatest side rejection, it picks up sounds from the rear more than a cardioid does.

Bidirectional/Figure Eight

A bidirectional mic (also called figure eight) picks up sound from the front and rear while it rejects sounds from the sides. These mics have a proximity effect that's approximately 6 dB greater than a cardioid mic.

Hemispherical/Boundary/PZM

The hemisphere or boundary mic is an omnidirectional mic that's mounted very close to a reflective surface, so that the distance between the mic and the surface is less that the wavelength of its highest pickup frequency. One of the best known types is marketed by Crown under their trade name Pressure Zone Microphone or PZM. Other manufacturers call their versions boundary or surface mount mics.

Most boundary mics are easily recognizable by their flat design, which is intended to be surface mounted to an instrument, table, wall, or floor. Since the pickup pattern is a hemisphere—like a ball that's been cut in half—the mic picks up all frequencies equally well in any direction above the surface on which it's mounted. These mics become directional at high frequencies if the surface is small while larger surfaces display a more uniform low-frequency response.

Boundary mics—nearly always condensers—are versatile, sound good, and can be used in many applications. They're often used on the stage for concert recording, on a table for conferences, on a piano lid, or on a studio wall for picking up ambient sounds.

Multi-Directional

Many studio condenser mics let you select between several pattern types, using a switch located on the mic or power supply. Getting used to the sound of a good multidirectional mic and learning how to use its various patterns helps you reduce the number of mics you need in your arsenal; they are simply more flexible and easily adapt to many situations that might be thrown your way.

Transient Response

A significant piece of data that has no presently-accepted standard is the transient response of a microphone. Transient response is the measure of how rapidly a microphone's diaphragm reacts to a sound wave that hits it, along with the resulting audible effect.

The transient response of a mic can alter its characteristic sound, since the instantaneous rise time of a signal might be shorter than the microphone's ability to accurately track the sound's complex impulse structure. For example, the rise times of speech and music are 10–100 milliseconds (ms), while the rise time of a high quality condenser mic is typically less than 1 ms. This ability to closely follow the waveform shape is what allows condenser mics to grasp the complex and delicate nature of sound.

Here's a breakdown of how the various mic types react to transient energy.

- Dynamic mics have a large diaphragm that has a metal wound coil attached to it. This large mass offers a great deal of resistance to being moved quickly, and thus to accurately tracking the acoustic pressure wave. In effect, this resistance to fast-acting pressure changes introduces a form of distortion into a dynamic's characteristic sound—a sound which tends to be rather gutsy, lacking high-end clarity and brilliance. Don't be fooled into thinking that this is a put-down: it's not! In many situations, this gutsy rugged sound is just what the doctor ordered.
- The ribbon mic has a much lighter diaphragm, and as such has much less mass than the dynamic mic. This almost always translates into improved transient response: the ribbon can capture sound with a greater degree of clarity and openness. This transient clarity is often mellowed by the protective grill that's needed to shield the diaphragm from excessive and potentially damaging windblasts. This mellowness has given this mic its "croony" reputation and makes it a good choice for vocals, horns and a host of other applications. This particularly holds true for older ribbon types.
- The diaphragm of the condenser mic has, by far, the least mass of all professional pickups. As such, its transient response is generally excellent. Condensers provide an open sonic character that's known for it's ability to accurately pickup sharp transients, with a crisp open sound that spans across the entire audible spectrum (CD Track 4).

Wind Protection and Protective Grill

Although you won't read this in a magazine article, many engineers are aware of the effect that a mic's windscreen and protective metal mesh grill can have on a mic's overall sonic character. By protective grill, we're referring to the metal outer casing—the cage—that protects a mic's diaphragm from being bashed by a fall or unsuspecting drum stick. Wind screen refers to the foam and fabric mesh that often protects a diaphragm from wind blasts and spit.

Over the years, it's become obvious that the larger cages and protective screens that cover many condenser, ribbon and even certain dynamics play a strong part in the shaping of a mic's character. This is total speculation on our part, but the sonic mellowing that occurs on mics that have these large mesh designs might be attributed to the reflection of high-frequencies off the case, as well as to the phase cancellation of high-frequencies within the casings themselves. You can either believe this or not; all we ask is that you keep in mind the possibility that this can be a determining factor.

Electrical Specifications

The electrical characteristics of a microphone refer to a specific model's measured output response to sensitivity, equivalent noise, overload characteristics, and impedance.

Sensitivity

Sensitivity is the output level that a microphone produces (in volts) when fed a standardized sound pressure level signal (generally 74 or 94 dB SPL). This spec tells the amount of amplification that's required to raise the microphone's relatively low output signal to a standard operating line level. This value also lets you judge the output level differences between two mics that are driven by the same acoustic input signal; a mic that has higher sensitivity will produce a stronger output voltage than a mic with lower sensitivity.

Many new mics have greater sensitivities and therefore higher output levels than older ones. Ribbon mics generally have lower sensitivity than dynamic and condenser mics; small diaphragm condensers often have lower output levels than their larger diaphragm counterparts. Some mic preamps, that have more than enough gain for a condenser or dynamic mic, might not be able to amplify ribbon mics without raising the preamp's noise to an unacceptable level.

Signal Overload

Sound pressure level (SPL) is a reference standard that essentially indicates how loud a sound is in dB; high SPLs can cause a mic to distort. The ability of a microphone to handle high SPLs without distortion is determined, primarily, by its construction.

Dynamic mics usually can handle high SPLs at levels reaching 140 dB or more. Ribbon mics are the most affected by high SPLs; too high a level could destroy the ribbon in some models.

The diaphragm of most condenser microphones generally won't distort, except under the most severe sound pressure levels. However, the condenser system differs from the dynamic system in that, at high acoustic levels, the capsule's output signal could be strong enough to overload the capsule's built-in preamp. To prevent this, many condenser mics let you insert an attenuation pad into the circuit by simply flipping a switch. When inserting the pad, keep in mind that the signal-to-noise ratio of the device is degraded by the amount of attenuation; thus, under normal SPL conditions it's wise to remove the pad.

Noise

A mic, like nearly all electronic devices, generates noise. The amount is usually way below the noise level of the console's amplification stages and analog tape. It usually isn't a factor when recording loud or moderately loud sound sources. However, microphone noise can be a problem in making digital recordings of soft sound sources. Manufacturers are aware of this problem and many mics are now advertised as having low noise.

A Few Cabling Considerations

Sometimes, mics are only as good as the cables that carry their signal. Problems with improperly wired or shielded cables can wreak absolute havoc with a mic's low-level signal. These problems could range from the mic not working at all, to gremlin noises that can make your hair stand on end. The following are a few considerations that should always be taken into account by a recording facility, no matter how small.

Cable Polarity

When more than one microphone is present in a system, the polarity of all microphones and cables must be standardized. Polarity is the phase relationship between the motion of a mic's diaphragm and its output voltage. When two or more microphones are placed near a sound source, each microphone receives a portion of the sound, possibly in the form of leakage. If the audio leads of any of these microphones are reversed, it is likely that signal phase cancellations could result, causing degradations in frequency response or complete electrical cancellation when combined into mono. To eliminate this possibility, all microphone cables must be properly phased at the connector ends. The polarity of the connector leads can be readily checked with an ohm meter or commercial phase checker. Simply use this meter or box to see that pin 1 of the connector, on one end of the cable, is connected to pin 1 on the other end, pin 2 to pin 2, and pin 3 to pin 3.

Undesirable phase interaction can be caused by mic placement, even though all cables are wired correctly and the mics themselves are otherwise in phase. This happens when the mics are positioned so the sound arrives at one mic out-of-phase with the same sound picked up by the other mic. This condition can be fixed with the phase switch on the console (if it has one), by replacing an improperly wired cable with a cable of proper polarity, or by using a phase reversal adapter.

A check of polarity differences between two mics can be made by panning both mics to mono, bringing up the level of one mic, and then slowly bringing up the level of the other mic. If the bass level goes down as the level of the second mic is increased, the mics are out of phase with each other.

Phantom Power

While early condenser mics and those with tube preamplifiers require their own separate power supply, most condenser mics today operate on phantom power. Most consoles have microphone phantom power built in, which can be applied to the microphone jacks by simply throwing a switch. External phantom power supplies for one or several microphones are readily available and can be used when the console doesn't supply phantom power. Most condenser mics operate on a phantom power of 48 Vdc, some operate on less, and others operate over a wide range of voltages (typically 9–48 Vdc). Typical phantom power specifications are 48 ±4 V, at a maximum of 2 milliamps [mA] or 12 ±1 V, at a maximum of 10 mA. Before applying phantom power to a condenser mic, check its specifications to see if it is matched with your phantom power supply (Figure 2-6).

In phantom powering, both the audio signal and the DC powering voltage are carried by the two conductors on the same balanced mic cable. A positive voltage is supplied to both microphone audio leads (XLR pins 2 and 3) through a set of matched value resistors (6.8 k ohm at 48 V, 1%, 1/4 W and 680 ohm at 12 V, 1%, 1/4 W) or via a transformer center tap. The negative side of the supply is returned to the power supply ground via the cable shield.

This powering method doesn't interfere with the normal operation of moving-coil or electret-condenser microphones since the positive voltage is equally applied to both signal leads.

Most consoles and mixers let you switch the phantom power off, either system-wide or on each input strip, because phantom powering might destroy the element of a ribbon microphone. For this reason, it's wise to switch the phantom power supply off when using a ribbon mic.

Phantom power can be used with some modern ribbon mics along with condensers but first check with the microphone manufacturer.

Figure 2-6
Phantom Power

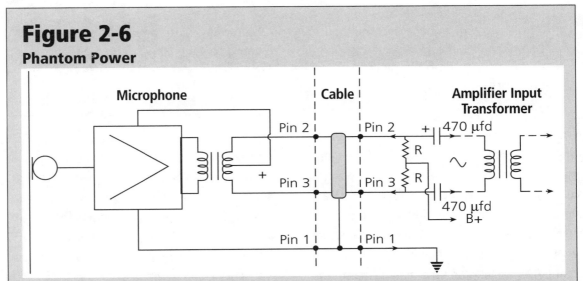

"...both the audio signal and the DC powering voltage are carried by the two conductors on the same balanced mic cable. A positive voltage is supplied to both microphone audio leads (XLR pins 2 and 3) through a set of matched value resistors (6.8 k ohm at 48 V, 1%, 1/4 W and 680 ohm at 12 V, 1%, 1/4 W) or via a transformer center tap. The negative side of the supply is returned to the power supply ground via the cable shield.

This powering method doesn't interfere with the normal operation of moving-coil or electret-condenser microphones since the positive voltage is equally applied to both signal leads."

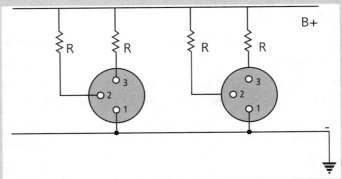

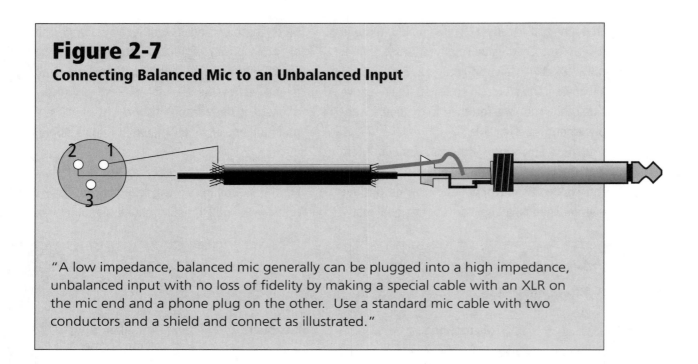

Figure 2-7
Connecting Balanced Mic to an Unbalanced Input

"A low impedance, balanced mic generally can be plugged into a high impedance, unbalanced input with no loss of fidelity by making a special cable with an XLR on the mic end and a phone plug on the other. Use a standard mic cable with two conductors and a shield and connect as illustrated."

Beyer ribbon mics, in particular, won't be damaged by correctly applied phantom power (at least, according to the manufacturer). Older vintage ribbon mics sometimes have a grounded transformer center tap and will be destroyed by phantom power. If a ribbon is used in a phantom power system, and the manufacturer says it won't be damaged, it's very important to see that the cable has all the connector pins connected properly: 1 to 1, 2 to 2, and 3 to 3. If the pin connections aren't the same throughout the phantom power run, the ribbon mic will just blow out like a big fuse.

Some condenser mics can be operated from a DC battery source. A few condenser microphone systems, such as the Neumann U-87 and AKG C1000, can work on internal batteries or phantom powering. Such a mic can be incorporated into any system without the need for an external power supply. External battery packs can be purchased or designed for powering one or more microphones, as long as the microphone's voltage requirements are met. Most externally powered condenser mics are designed to operate at the nominal range (48 ±4 V). Should a lower potential, such as 12 V, be applied, degradation in distortion, noise and frequency response figures can occur.

Connecting Balanced to Unbalanced

There are two ways of connecting a balanced mic or line source into an unbalanced input: using a transformer, or building a special cable. The best way is to use a balanced to unbalanced transformer. Several companies make transformer adapters with a female XLR on one end and a phone plug on the other. The XLR end is connected to the mic with a standard balanced mic cable. The transformer's primary side matches the impedance of the mic and is balanced, while the secondary is unbalanced and has a high impedance that matches most unbalanced preamps.

A low impedance, balanced mic generally can be plugged into a high impedance, unbalanced input with no loss of fidelity by making a special cable with an XLR on the mic end and a phone plug on the other. Use a standard mic cable with two conductors and a shield and connect as illustrated (Figure 2-7).

To connect an unbalanced mic to a balanced input, where the mic has a cable with a center conductor and a shield, wire the shield to pins 1 and 3 of the XLR and the center wire to pin 2 (Figure 2-8).

Radio Frequency (Rf) Interference

The purpose of the grounded shield in a signal cable is to reduce the pickup of extraneous electrostatic noise such as the dreaded radio frequency interference—RFI for short. An improperly grounded audio cable or circuit can be an excellent antenna for radio waves. These low-level modulated radio signals can then be amplified by an unbalanced input stage as an audible signal—commonly your least favorite radio station or citizen's band buddy. Electrostatic pickup also can be caused by electronically controlled lighting systems like those used at rock concerts.

Radio frequency interference can be reduced in several ways. The best of these is to use sets of properly grounded, balanced lines throughout your production setup. Whenever possible, mic cables should be physically separated from higher-level power cords and grids. For example, in a permanent installation, where high power fields exist, consider a common ground system where all the mic cables are electrostatically shielded within runs of metal conduit.

RFI sometimes makes its way into condenser mics, especially those with transformerless output circuits. In these cases, the mic

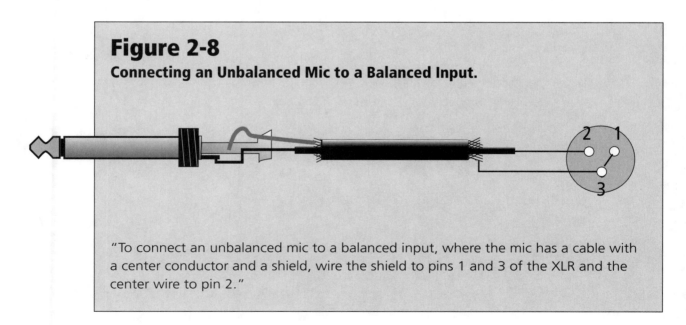

Figure 2-8
Connecting an Unbalanced Mic to a Balanced Input.

"To connect an unbalanced mic to a balanced input, where the mic has a cable with a center conductor and a shield, wire the shield to pins 1 and 3 of the XLR and the center wire to pin 2."

cable's ground connection is often the problem. In many preamps, the ground pin (pin 1) on the circuit board's connector doesn't provide an adequate ground. The remedy is to use a male XLR on the mic cable where the ground lug has been soldered to pin 1 of the cable's XLR. Provided that the XLR's shell is solidly grounded to the preamp's chassis, this fix can help adequately ground the cable shield to avoid RFI. Sometimes the cable shield must be attached to the shell on both ends of the cable, instead of just on the male connector end. Also, some condenser mics draw more current from the phantom supply than the small circuit trace that connects pin 1 to the preamp can handle. Grounding the shell of the mic cable to pin 1 and the cable shield often solves this problem.

Chapter 3 Basic Microphone Techniques

As you've read from the previous chapter, mics come in all shapes, sounds, operating types, and pickup patterns. The question of which type of mic to use for a particular application has been the subject of many a career.

Just as the path to Carnegie Hall is through practice—lots of practice—knowing how to best use microphones comes from insights learned by applying the mic techniques you learn. The following are a number of guidelines that can help you make the right choices.

The Recording Environment

Before you begin recording, it's always a good idea to size up your recording environment, comparing it to how the instrument and type of music should relate to that environment. What I mean by this is:

- Figure out if the room sounds good—or does it sound crappy, coloring the recorded sound. If the room doesn't sound good, try to figure out why. Is the room too live with too many resonances? Try laying down carpets and/or pulling the drapes. If you want to keep the room sounding relatively live, you can also use sonic separators (a.k.a., flats or gobos) at an angle to absorb reflections and to break up some of the opposing reflective surfaces.
- If the room still doesn't sound good, you always have the option of placing the mics closer to the sound sources to reduce the amount of room sound that's being picked up—or you could simply record elsewhere.
- If the room does sound good, will the instruments sound good in it? Is it too live for drums or too dead for strings? Will the instrument(s) fit into the room? If you run into a size or sonic snag, fear not: you might try recording in your living room, garage, a professional studio or you could possibly beg, borrow and steal the concert venue that's owned by your best friend's boss to overdub an instrument. If the room sounds good and seems to work …roll the tape!

We've always been big proponents of the idea that you don't always need to spend big bucks to get a great sound: this is, of course, the whole idea behind the home project studio. Rooms come in all shapes and sizes, as well as dollars and cents. One of the most logical approaches to a recording room that works for a wide variety of applications is to make the room as versatile and cost effective as possible. For example, taking a room that's relatively reflective in nature—as most living spaces are—and laying down carpets or pulling drapes to deaden the sound can be a lot easier and cheaper than starting with an acoustically dead room and adding reflective surfaces for a specific session. In short, having a room that looks, feels, and sounds comfortable often works better than a room that's been transformed into a hodge-podge of acoustic stuff.

In the end, probably the most important thing that can be said is, "Don't be afraid of recording in a room." It's entirely possible that the idea that a room has to be acoustically perfect is more of a marketing ploy by the trade mags and designers than a major factor in creating a successful recording. In this light, the real aim of a room is to:

- Create an acoustic space that's live enough so the musicians can hear themselves.
- Create an acoustic space that's dead enough to provide adequate isolation between instruments and/or mics: if this is a problem, you can use acoustic separators, such as flats or blankets. If at all possible, try to place the musicians and/or separators so the musicians can see and hear each other, as well as themselves: this can be accomplished acoustically and/or via headphones.
- Create a space that's true to the musical style if size and room reflections are part of the music, (i.e., classical).
- Create an acoustic space that's sufficiently isolated from outside noises that could make it onto tape.
- Be comfortable! This includes having adequate or appropriate lighting, a good monitor mix through the headphones, adequate ventilation, coffee, tea and thee.

Many of these requirements can be carried out in a wide variety of acoustic spaces such as recording studios, project studios, warehouse spaces, living rooms, and bedrooms; it simply comes down to the scope, the size and the budget of the session. To repeat this goal in one short and sweet phrase: Use your skills and intuition to size up the room and to match the room to the needs to the musician, the instrument, the mic, and the music.

Microphone Placement

Mic placement is a subjective art form. Although guidelines have their place in the professional media, what might be considered to be a really bad technique now could easily be the fad of the future. As new music styles and equipment develop, sound recording techniques will evolve—or come back into vogue. Basically, as with any art form, the techniques and technology of miking are constantly being kept alive by innovation and experimentation. The rest of this chapter is, therefore, dedicated to helping you develop guidelines for creating your own techniques by describing the many choices of single microphone technique used today. By the single microphone technique, we're referring to the pickup of a sound source by a single mono mic. Later on, in Chapter 6, you can examine other techniques in the form of stereo placement.

Sound Characteristics as a Function of Working Distance

In modern studio and sound stage recording, four basic styles of microphone placement are directly related to the distance of a microphone from its sound source. These are: close-miking, accent-miking, distant-miking and ambient-miking.

Close Microphone Placement

Close-miking techniques refer to placing the mic at a distance of about one inch to three feet away from the sound source. It can safely be said that this is the most commonly used tech-

Figure 3-1
Controlling Leakage

Here are a few options that can be used to reduce leakage:

- In moderation, physically separate the sound sources. This works because sound—and thus leakage—drops six dB in level as miking distance is doubled.

- Place the involved mics closer to their respective sound sources. In this way, the direct sound level increases relative to the unwanted leakage. Remember, try to maintain a good tonal balance as this distance is decreased.

- Use directional mics. A directional microphone favors on-axis sounds while it discriminates against unwanted off-axis leakage.

- Isolate the sound sources by placing an acoustic barrier known as a flat or gobo between them. Placing the objectionable source in another room—often known as an isolation booth, iso booth or iso room—can achieve the same results.

In addition to these options, if the source signal is electric you can eliminate the obtrusive acoustic source by recording its signal directly onto tape and bypassing the mic, or by overdubbing the louder instrument at a later time onto a separate track. Both of these options reduce leakage, as the softer instrument could then be recorded without any acoustic interference.

nique in modern-day project and studio multi-track music production. Close-miking serves two major functions:

1. It gives the sound a tight, present quality.
2. It effectively excludes the acoustic environment from being picked up.

Because sound diminishes with the square of its distance, a sound originating six feet from a mic is insignificant in level when compared to the level of the same sound that originates three inches from it. As a result, only the desired on-axis sound will be recorded onto tape while, for all practical purposes, extraneous sounds won't be picked up.

Although close-miking has its advantages, a mic should be placed only as close to the source as is necessary, not as close as is possible.

Miking too close can definitely color the recorded tone quality of a source. Since these techniques generally involve distances of 1–6 inches, the entire tonal balance (timbre) of a sound source stands a good chance of not being picked up. Rather, the mic is now placed so close that only a small portion of the sound surface is actually heard by the mic, giving an area-specific pickup balance. At these close distances, moving a mic only a few inches changes the overall tonal balance of the pickup. Three remedies are available:

1. Move the mic along the surface of the instrument's source until you get the sound you want.
2. Place the mic at a greater distance from the sound source so as to widen the pick up angle and thus pickup more of the instrument's

overall sound.

3. Equalize the signal until a desired balance is achieved.

Leakage

The basic premise of the multitrack recording process is to get control over each sound source by having a moderate-to-high degree of isolation between sources. Should a mic pick up an extraneous instrument or sound that's recording adjacent to the source, a condition known as leakage occurs. Since the pickup contains a mixture of both the direct and indirect signals, changing the track's level during mixdown would also affect the level and sound character of the instrument that's leaking into that track. Because

excessive leakage tends to make a sound track more live and less intelligible, it's generally avoided (Figure 3-1).

Phase Problems as a Result of Leakage

Sometimes, more than one mic is used to pick up a single sound source—as when miking a drum set—to produce an immediate sound that's often larger than life. When using this technique, phase cancellation problems can be produced by using too many mics that are placed too far from the sound source, a condition that can result in excess leakage and a degraded pickup response. Should a single sound source be picked up by two nearby microphones at

Figure 3-2
3:1 Principle

In order to avoid acoustical phase cancellations, a quick-n-easy guideline called the 3:1 principle can be used. This principle states: In order to maintain phase integrity between two or more mics, for every unit of distance between each mic and its source, the distance between mics should be at least three times that mic-to-source distance. In addition to this guideline, you might want to keep in mind that it's often unnecessary to use more than one mic in a pickup area where a single mic would give adequate, if not better coverage.

When close-miking an instrument with more than one mic, you should also make sure that the mics are electrically in phase with each other. If this isn't the case, the problem might simply be a mis-wired cable, creating signal cancellations at various frequencies. This can be easily solved by:

- Replacing the cable with one that's properly phased

- Repairing the cable to its proper polarity of pin 2 (+) and 3 (-) on an XLR connector by soldering the reversed leads (you can use a polarity tester to find out which one's bad)

- Reversing the polarity on the console's input strip—if a polarity switch is available

- Reversing the cable to its proper polarity by inserting a phase-reversal adapter

roughly an equal intensity, variations in phase could result from the differing path lengths, and thus time, as they travel to both mics. Once these signals are combined to a single channel, a single track, or are listened to in mono, cancellations can occur, producing severe frequency response dips in the recorded sound (Figure 3-2).

Distant Microphone Placement

Distant-miking refers to the placement of one or more microphones about three or more feet from a sound source. This technique serves two functions:

1. It places the mic at such a distance that an entire musical instrument or ensemble is picked up, thus preserving the overall tonal

Figure 3-3
Distant-miking

"Distant-miking is often used to pickup a balance between an instrument (or instrumental ensemble) and its acoustic environment. This balance can be determined by a number of factors, including the size of the instrument or sound source and the reverberant characteristic of the room.

These techniques tend to add a live, airy, or open feeling to a recording because distant microphones cover a larger portion of the acoustic soundfield—meaning that fewer mics are used to cover a wide pickup angle."

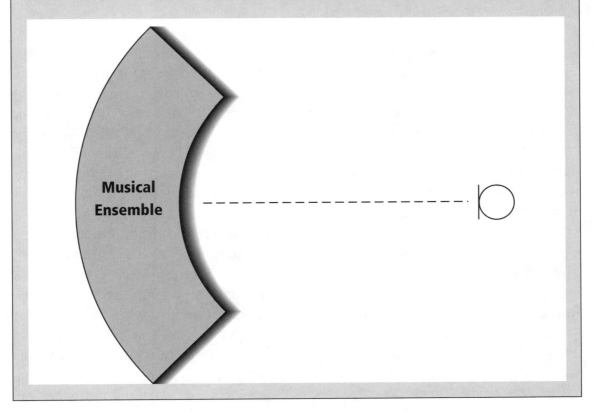

Musical Ensemble

balance of that instrument or ensemble. A natural tonal balance can often be achieved by placing the microphone at a distance that's roughly equal to the size of the sound radiating surface of the instrument or sound source.

2. It places the mic at enough of a distance that the acoustic environment is included within its pickup and thus is combined with the direct signal of the sound source (Figure 3-3).

Distant-miking is often used to pickup a balance between an instrument (or instrumental ensemble) and its acoustic environment. This balance can be determined by a number of factors, including the size of the instrument or sound source and the reverberant characteristic of the room.

These techniques tend to add a live, airy, or open feeling to a recording because distant microphones cover a larger portion of the acoustic soundfield—meaning that fewer mics are used to cover a wide pickup angle.

One of the potential drawbacks to distant-miking is that the acoustic environment might not be very good; bad room reflections and/or a discolored sound, due to phase cancellations at various frequencies, could be picked up, creating a muddy or poorly defined recording. To avoid this problem, you can:

- Temporarily correct for reflections by using absorptive or offset reflective panels
- Place the microphone closer to its source and add artificial reverberation if needed

Accent Microphone Placement

As we saw earlier, both distant- and close-miking offer entirely different pickup and tonal qualities. Under certain circumstances, it's difficult to get a natural recorded balance when mixing these two techniques. For example, the classical symphonic recording styles rely upon distant mic techniques to provide a natural balance between direct and reverberant (ambient) sound. Should a solo instrumental passage occur in the score, an additional microphone might be needed to adequately pick it up; however, if the solo instrument is miked too closely, the instrument can sound too present and "out of context" with the overall distant pickup. To help the pickup sound more natural, a compromise in distance—and thus pickup balance—must be struck between a close and distant placement point. A microphone that's placed within this compromised range is known as an accent microphone (Figure 3-4).

When using an accent microphone, choose your mic placement, and the amount that's blended into the overall mix, carefully. Quite simply, it shouldn't discolor or change the balance of the soloist to the other surrounding instruments within the stereo perspective. Good accent-mic technique only adds presence to the sound of a solo passage and shouldn't be perceived as a separate pickup. Careful and appropriate panning of an accent mic into the overall stereo image helps eliminate any wandering images that might occur with changes in solo intensity.

Ambient Microphone Placement

When a mic is placed at enough of a distance that a room's reverberant sound dominates over the direct signal, that mic is said to be an ambient pickup. Either one or two mics can be used to pick up a room's ambience. For example, a single omnidirectional mic can be placed out into the room to pickup the natural reflections (Figure 3-5, Mic 1) or two spaced or coincident cardioids can be placed into the room, facing away from the direct sound (Figure 3-5, Mic Setup 2). Another method that works extremely well is to place two coincident mics in the Blumlein

- In a live concert recording, ambient microphones can be placed in the room to pickup the audience's reaction and applause.
- In a studio recording, ambient microphones

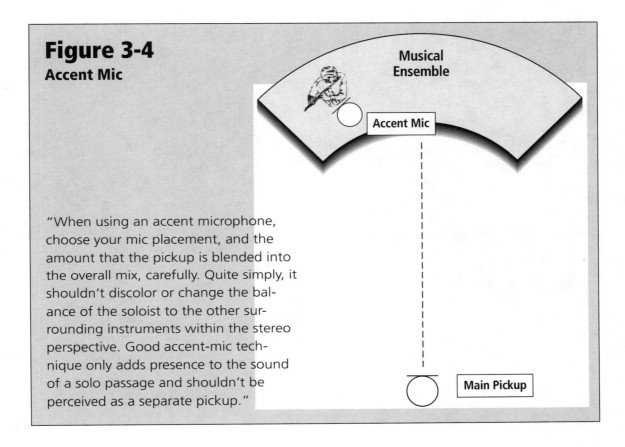

Figure 3-4
Accent Mic

Musical
Ensemble

Accent Mic

Main Pickup

"When using an accent microphone, choose your mic placement, and the amount that the pickup is blended into the overall mix, carefully. Quite simply, it shouldn't discolor or change the balance of the soloist to the other surrounding instruments within the stereo perspective. Good accent-mic technique only adds presence to the sound of a solo passage and shouldn't be perceived as a separate pickup."

crossed figure eight pattern (See Chapter 6) into the room (Figure 3-5, Mics 3 and 4). Any of these pickups can be used on their own to give a distant spacious effect, or they can be mixed in with close-placed microphones to give a sense of spaciousness to a mix.

An ambient microphone can be used in any situation to enhance a recording, such as:

- In a live concert recording, ambient microphones can be placed in the hall to restore the natural reverberation that might be lost with the use of close-miking techniques.

can be used to give a mix a fuller, more spacious sound. Ambient-miking can also be used as an effect, adding depth to a sound; for example, if a previously recorded track is played loudly over a set of studio/stage monitors and is then rerecorded by a pair of ambient mics, you might come up with a fatter and larger sound which can then be blended with the original signal.

Although we've dealt separately with close, distant, accent, and ambient placement techniques, any of these can be mixed and

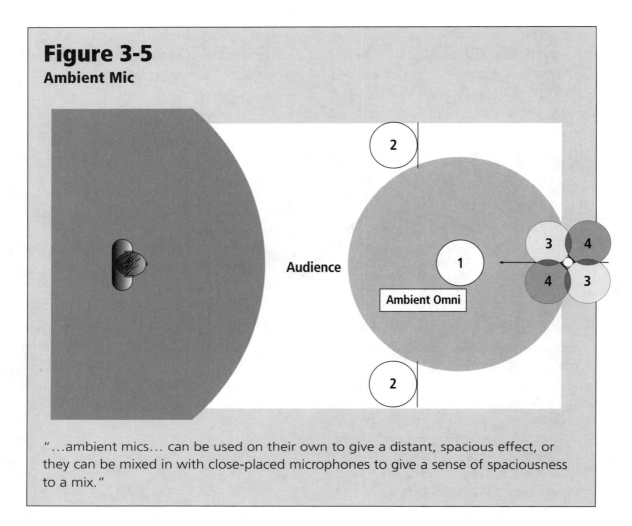

Figure 3-5
Ambient Mic

Audience

1

Ambient Omni

2

2

3 4

4 3

"…ambient mics… can be used on their own to give a distant, spacious effect, or they can be mixed in with close-placed microphones to give a sense of spaciousness to a mix."

matched to your experimental heart's content—as long as the production style fits the type of music or other source being recorded. For example, distant-mic techniques aren't, by any means, limited to classical music, as is sometimes believed. The sound of a jazz flute can sound interesting whether it's recorded in the studio at a distance of one foot or in the Taj Mahal at 50 feet. Through experimentation and proper forethought, the blending of these techniques can create some rather wild and unique effects.

Chapter 4 Miking Instruments

Now, we get to the good stuff. This chapter details various miking techniques for most of the instruments that you might encounter during a typical—or not-so-typical—session. The instruments are listed alphabetically, each one giving you a number of techniques to help you get professional results as quickly as possible, with the least amount of fuss. In addition, the illustrations will often include several placements that can be easily identified by number.

These practical methods are designed to realistically capture the sound of the instrument without undue coloration. In most cases, the primary focus is on single microphone techniques, whereby a single mic is amplified, processed and routed to a single track of a multitrack recorder; however, techniques that use more than one microphone are also described where appropriate.

Accordion

This lively instrument comes in several sizes and styles, and can pop up in many different types of music in a number of ways. The accordion family makes its sound by using bellows to force air through tuned metal reeds. Its pickup often uses two mics, since most have a treble side located to the listener's left—where the melody is played—and a bass side (the right-most side)

which is reserved for bass notes and/or chord accompaniment. Obviously, these two sides can be recorded in stereo for that panavision effect, or they can be combined together into mono.

Accordions tend to make mechanical noise from the keys and the constant action of the bellows. In some forms of music, these mechanical noises are considered to be part of the musical idiom; in other types these sounds aren't wanted and distant-miking techniques must be used to minimize them.

It's important when recording instruments of the accordion family to understand the musical idiom that's being recorded and to accommodate the needs of the style. It's also essential that you work with the performer to get a clear understanding of what should be heard in the recording. It may take some experimentation to find the proper mic placement and tracking technique for the instrument; however, due to the wide range of differences between accordions and types of music played on them, the accordion can be a challenging instrument to record.

It's generally preferable to use two microphones, one pointed at the keyboard (right hand) side to pick up the melody and one pointed at the bass side (left hand) to pick up the bass (Figure 4-1, Mic Setup 1, CD Track 5). These mics are recorded onto two tracks and blended in the mix for monaural or sometimes panned for stereo. If a natural sound is the goal, care has to be taken that the stereo sound is not made too large by hard panning left and right. Sound comes from the entire height of the instrument so the mics need to be placed at a sufficient distance to pick up all the reeds evenly.

If the sound of the instrument's mechanics are desired, such as in traditional recordings, the mic should be placed as close as possible while still achieving good balance from one end of the fingerboard to the other. For a standard piano accordion, a close-miked distance of 12 inches from the treble and the bass end of the instrument is a good place to start. Keep in mind that the player is moving the bellows in and out, so place the mics accordingly. During an overdub, moving the treble and bass mics out to about three to four feet will provide a more even balance and minimize mechanical noises.

A single mic with a wide pickup pattern, such as a large-diaphragm cardioid or omnidirectional condenser, will give good results when positioned a foot or so in front of the instrument pointing midway between the bellows (Figure 4-1, Mic 2, CD Track 5).

Accordion Tip
Accordions can produce high signal levels when close-miked, so listen carefully for mic overload and use the mic's pad whenever necessary.

Figure 4-1
Accordion

"It's generally preferable to use two microphones, one pointed at the keyboard (right hand) side to pick up the melody and one pointed at the bass side (left hand) to pick up the bass."

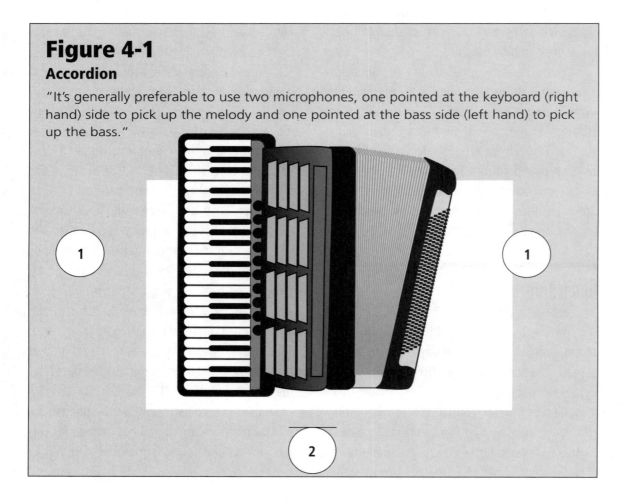

Bandoneon

The bandoneon is an Argentine button accordion that's used a lot in tangos. For recording, it can be thought of as a large concertina. The melody notes come from both right and left hand ends of the instrument. See the concertina discussion for tips on miking this instrument.

Button Accordion

There are many types of button accordions, ranging from multiple-row models which are the same size as a full-size piano accordion to single-row instruments that are only a foot or so high. Button accordions (also called a Melodeon) can be miked the same as a piano accordion; however, you should be aware of the type of music that's being played. Irish, English, and contra dance players use both the right and left sides of the instrument, generally with a more heavy emphasis on the melodic right hand side of the instrument. Often a satisfactory recording of these styles can be done with one broad pattern microphone placed in front of the instrument toward the treble side. Tex-Mex players, on the other hand, use only the right hand side of the instrument, so it's only necessary to mike the right side (Figure 4-1, Mic 1). Cajun and Zydeco players use both the right and left sides, so you should use two mics or one broad pattern mic that can pick up both sides with the proper balance. Often, button accordions in traditional music are miked at a greater distance, especially when they're part of an ensemble.

Concertina

Rather than having a treble and a bass side like most accordions, the concertina produces the melody line from both ends. However, since it's a small instrument, good recordings can be made by placing one mic about 10 inches directly in front or by placing an X-Y stereo pair about two feet in front of the player.

Autoharp

The autoharp is a zither-type instrument that's designed with chord bars that press down onto the strings, dampening all the strings except those that are part of the sounded chord. This quiet instrument is generally played by putting the instrument against the chest and resting the bottom in the crook of the left arm—a shoulder strap is often used to hold it up. The left hand is typically used to work the chord bars while the right hand picks or strums the instrument above the chord bars. Alternately, the autoharp can lay flat on the player's lap or a table while being strummed—often with a felt pick—below the chord bars (Figure 4-2).

Bagpipes

Bagpipes are encountered in many cultures. The best known are the highland pipes of Scotland and the UilleAnn pipes of Ireland. These instruments consist of a fingered chanter, on which the melody is played, and a set of drone pipes that are fastened into a bag which is filled with air.

The highland pipes are usually played standing up. The drone pipes point straight up and tower over the head of the player while the chanter is pointed down in front. The UilleAnn pipes often are played sitting down with the drone pipes pointing out to the side and the

Figure 4-2
Autoharp

Since It has a relatively low sound output, the autoharp should be miked at about 12" in front of the middle of the instrument using a broad frequency response pickup (Mic 1, CD Track 6). Getting adequate bass from an autoharp can be a challenge.

If the artist desires more bass, try using a lavaliere mic wrapped in foam pinned to the player's shirt at about the left-hand pocket level (Mic 2, CD Track 6). Feed this mic into a separate channel and blend it in with the front microphone as needed.

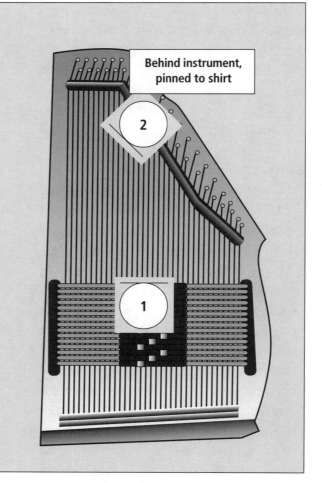

Behind instrument, pinned to shirt

chanter pointing down. It's important to pick up both the lead from the chanter and the drone notes from the drone pipes. This can be done effectively with one mic that's positioned to give the best balance between the lead and drone sounds.

Try a condenser mic at least two feet, and often up to eight feet or more, in front of the player, positioned in height to get a good balance between the lead and drone. A coincident stereo pair in this position works well for stereo. It's also possible to mic the chanter and the drones separately, using a cardioid close mic on the chanter aimed about 1/3 of the way up

from the bell at the lower finger holes, with another cardioid mic positioned above the drone pipes about two feet away. Bagpipes can be quite loud, possibly requiring that you use a pad on a condenser mic.

Banjo

The banjo has a head stretched across its body, much like a drum, that amplifies the string's vibrations. While containing strong fundamentals in the lower mid-frequency range, the complex harmonic structure of the banjo can easily continue upwards to 10 kHz. This, combined with a sharp transient quality, gives the banjo a clear and present sound. While all banjos are fundamentally the same, there are several different types and playing styles that require different miking techniques.

Banjos are built both with and without a resonator. Banjos with resonators generally have considerably more sound output than non-resonated instruments and could overload a microphone that's placed too close. There's also a marked difference in playing styles between those used in bluegrass (where the instrument is played by finger picking), folk (where the player might "hit down" on the strings with the fingernail, as in "clawhammer" old time playing) and Dixieland tenor or plectrum banjos (which are played with a flat pick). A flat

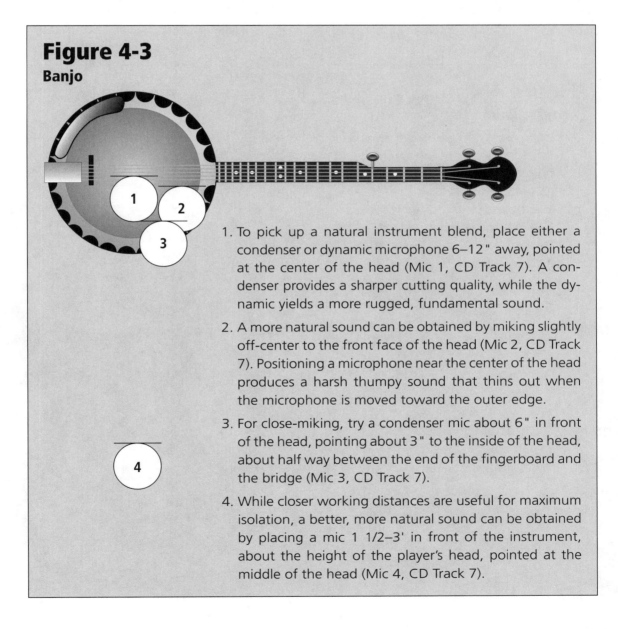

Figure 4-3
Banjo

1. To pick up a natural instrument blend, place either a condenser or dynamic microphone 6–12" away, pointed at the center of the head (Mic 1, CD Track 7). A condenser provides a sharper cutting quality, while the dynamic yields a more rugged, fundamental sound.

2. A more natural sound can be obtained by miking slightly off-center to the front face of the head (Mic 2, CD Track 7). Positioning a microphone near the center of the head produces a harsh thumpy sound that thins out when the microphone is moved toward the outer edge.

3. For close-miking, try a condenser mic about 6" in front of the head, pointing about 3" to the inside of the head, about half way between the end of the fingerboard and the bridge (Mic 3, CD Track 7).

4. While closer working distances are useful for maximum isolation, a better, more natural sound can be obtained by placing a mic 1 1/2–3' in front of the instrument, about the height of the player's head, pointed at the middle of the head (Mic 4, CD Track 7).

picked banjo often has considerably more percussive attack and output level than the more traditional, open-backed five-string banjo (Figure 4-3).

Banjo Tip

Banjos played with a plectrum, such as are used in jazz and Celtic music, can be quite loud with a strong transient attack, depending on the instrument and the playing style. Close-miking these instruments with a high quality condenser mic is desired to bring out this snap. Watch for mic overload and use the pad if necessary.

Basses

Acoustic Bass

The bass is one of lowest-pitched instruments. The four-string type reaches down to El (41 Hz) and the five-string to Cl (33 Hz) while the upper limit of the fundamental range is around middle

Figure 4-4
Acoustic bass

1. Most basses have a sweet spot a few inches up from the top of the f hole on the treble side. Listen in this area while the instrument is being played to find it. A mic placed 6"–3' in front of this spot will often produce the best sound (Mic 1, CD Track 8).

2. If it sounds too thin, try placing a second mic right over the f hole to pick up more bass, blending it with the more distant mic (Mic 2, CD Track 8).

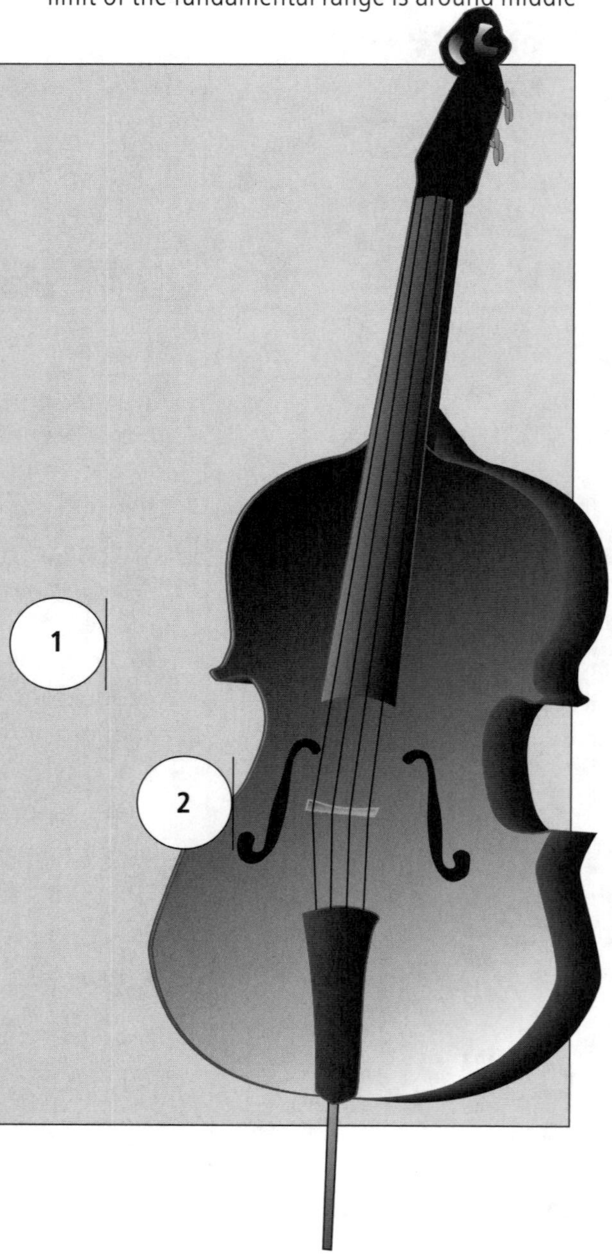

C (260 Hz). The instrument gets its rich, dark quality from frequencies that lie between 70 Hz and 250 Hz while frequencies below 70 Hz are naturally rolled off. The overtones generally reach up to 7 kHz; however, only a narrow band of frequencies (around 100 Hz) is radiated evenly in all directions. The angle of dispersion for all frequencies is roughly ±15° from the player's line of sight.

Acoustic Bass Tips

- The mic distance depends on the type of music and acoustic environment. In the classical playing style, the bass is usually bowed, which sets up strong buzzing sounds which contain frequency components up to 10 kHz. In jazz and folk, the bass is usually plucked and its overtones are weaker and fewer in number. In order to capture these subtle qualities, you might want to place the mics at shorter working distances.

- A wide range of microphones can be tried with the bass, including small and large diaphragm condensers, vocal dynamics and omnidirectional dynamics. A wide-range condenser microphone won't always produce the best recording. If you're not getting the results you want with a particular mic or technique, try a radically different one.

- The acoustic bass presents some unique difficulties as its sound radiates throughout the room and attention often must be paid to room acoustics and acoustic controls. Using gobos to surround the bass can minimize the effects of room reverberation. Sound absorbing baffles can also be improvised using quilts, mattresses and heavy blankets. Use a rug to minimize floor reflections. It is especially difficult to record a bass in ensemble with other instruments in a live recording.

Unless the bass is adequately baffled, or even in another room, there may be enough bass picked up by the other instrument mics to make it very difficult to get a good, punchy bass recording. Much better control over the bass recording can be achieved by overdubbing it all by itself.

- Since the notes of most acoustic and electric basses vary widely in level over the musical scale, it's a common practice for compression to be used to smooth out these variations in level. This practice also lets you turn the overall volume of the instrument up, giving it a punchier, more present sound. For tips on using compression and gating, see Chapter 7: *Outboard Stuff*.

- Many nonclassical bass players use a contact pickup or lapel mic for live performances. Depending upon the pickup type and placement, this method can yield results that range from not so great to in-yo-face fantastic.

Electric Bass

The electric bass guitar operates in the range of El to F4 (41.2 Hz to 343.2 Hz); however, if the player plays loudly or with a pick, the added harmonics could range up to 4 kHz. As you might expect, the playing style and choice of pickup will greatly affect the sound. Playing in the slap style or with a pick results in a brighter, harder attack while fingering the bass mellows the tone—which can be further deepened by pickup selection.

The electric bass can be recorded either by miking the speaker (Figure 4-5, CD Track 9) or by using a DI (direct injection box) to record directly from the pickup. The latter style will result in a cleaner, sharper attack and can solve some or all leakage problems when recording bass on stage or in a small studio space.

Electric Bass Tips

- Keeping the instrument levels high and the amp levels low generally results in a cleaner sound. Dynamic mics are usually chosen because of their deep rugged tone. Some large diaphragm dynamic designs subdue the high-frequency transients and, when combined with a boosted response around 100 Hz, give a warm mellow tone that is power-

ful in the lower register. Equalization of the bass signal may increase the clarity, with the fundamental being effected from 125–400 Hz and the harmonic punch being effected at 1.5–2 kHz.

- The electric bass records best when properly set up with a new set of strings, the pickup adjustment screws set for even output from all strings, and the intonation set so it plays in tune.

- As with the acoustic bass, using a compressor helps even out the note-to-note level

Figure 4-5
Electric bass

"…electric bass can be recorded either by miking the speaker (CD Track 9) or by using a DI (direct injection box) to record directly from the pickup. The latter style will result in a cleaner, sharper attack and can solve some or all leakage problems when recording bass on stage or in a small studio space."

Figure 4-6
Bassoon

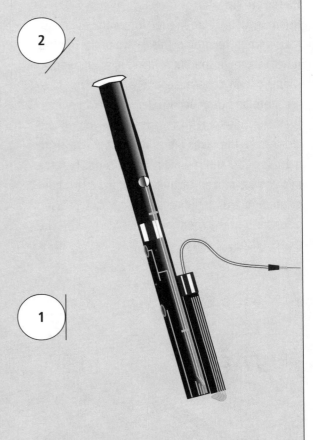

1. Because of its length, to achieve balanced pickup, the mic should have a broad pickup pattern and be placed far enough away to pick up the entire instrument evenly. Try a large diaphragm condenser mic placed 2–4' away, in either an omnidirectional or cardioid pattern, pointed at about the middle of the keys (Mic 1, CD Track 10). Again, use your ears and find a spot that gives good balance.

2. If isolation is needed to reduce leakage from other instruments, placing a mic or lapel mic near the instrument's bell will provide acceptable results (Mic 2, CD Track 10). You should be aware that all the sound doesn't come out of the bell; rather, the level of the notes tends to increase as they move down the scale. For this reason, a clip or lapel mic would do better than a standard mic as the low-end response tends to be rolled off. Using a compressor might help even out the note-to-note level differences that are often encountered when miking a woodwind bell (See Chapter 7: *Outboard Stuff*).

differences that are often encountered from the electric bass (See Chapter 7: *Outboard Stuff*).

Bassoon

The bassoon is the largest member of the woodwind family. There are two types in common orchestral use: the standard bassoon, which has its bell at the top—at or above the height of the player's head—and the contra or double bassoon, which plays its lowest note one octave below the standard bassoon. The latter has its bell pointing downward at about the height of the seated player's hips.

The sound from this deep and mellow instrument radiates from the its entire length, with the strongest sound coming from the lowest open finger hole. The lowest note on a standard bassoon is around 60 Hz and on a contrabassoon, 30 Hz.

Bassoon Tip

Room resonance and reflections can be a major factor when recording this instrument. The low notes can set up standing waves in an undamped room, which can cause one or more notes to resonate and be much louder, and less defined, than the others. If this is the case, you should close-mike the instrument. If the room environment is good and room ambience is desired, the mic can be moved farther from the instrument or an ambient omnidirectional mic can be used elsewhere in the room and blended in with the closer pickup.

Bodhran

The Bodhran is a two feet in diameter, open backed drum with a relatively shallow wooden rim which is held in the hand and played with a beater. Although it's similar in design to many Native American drums, this rowdy and loud instrument is primarily used in Irish music.

Since the bodhran often has a pronounced low end boom, you'll want to use a mic that can handle the SPLs. One of the best techniques is to close-mike it 6–18 inches in front of the rim with the bass roll-off switched on at the mic or on the console's input strip. The roll-off will help you minimize the boom, which obscures the

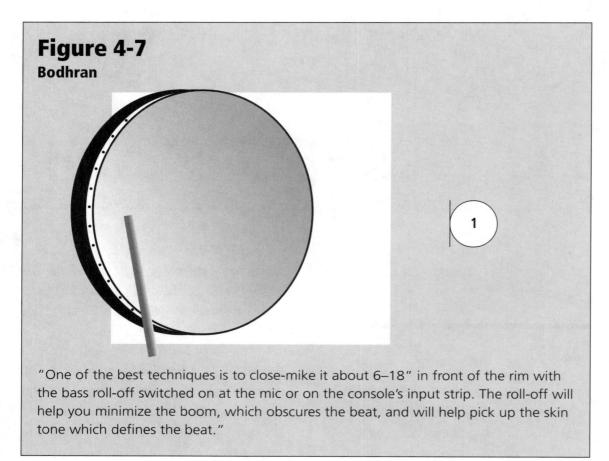

Figure 4-7
Bodhran

1

"One of the best techniques is to close-mike it about 6–18" in front of the rim with the bass roll-off switched on at the mic or on the console's input strip. The roll-off will help you minimize the boom, which obscures the beat, and will help pick up the skin tone which defines the beat."

beat, and will help pick up the skin tone, which defines the beat. In recording a live ensemble, the bodhran may need to be acoustically isolated to prevent too much boom from leaking into the other microphones (CD Track 11).

Bodhran Tip

Large diaphragm condenser and dynamic mics generally work well. Compression can be used to even out the level variations and to bring out more punch.

Bouzouki

The bouzouki is a Greek instrument that's built like a lute with a long neck. From an acoustic standpoint, you can get good results by using the same technique that's used to pick up the mandolin. Often, electric pickups are an integral part of the sound for some types of bouzouki music. As such, you might have to treat the bouzouki as an electric instrument. In either case, you should talk with the player to determine the desired sound.

Cello

The fundamental range of the cello lies from C2 to C5, corresponding to a frequency range of 56 to 520 Hz, with an overtone spectrum that rises to 8 kHz. Most important are the "o" formants that lie between 350 Hz and 600 Hz, which combine to create the cello's sonorous character. If we assume the player's line of sight is 0°, the preferred direction of sound radiation

Figure 4-8
Cello

Place the mic level with the instrument directed toward the treble f hole. The mic—usually a condenser or extended range dynamic—should have a flat response and be placed between 6 and 8' away (Mic 1, CD Track 12). Miking at a closer distance produces a more present sound with less leakage from other instruments, but won't pick up the whole instrument. Moving the mic back will pick up more of the entire instrument, but will include more leakage and more of the room environment. Generally, classical cello should be miked at a greater distance than cellos that are used in popular or folk music (Mic 2, CD Track 12).

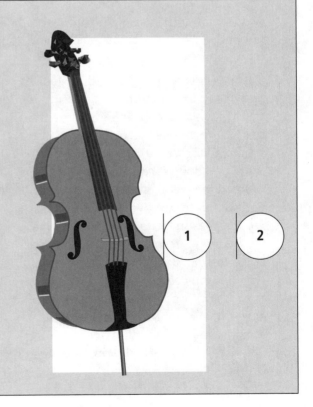

lies between 10 and 45° to the right of the instrument (Figure 4-8).

Clarinet

The clarinet comes in two pitches: the B flat clarinet with a lower limit of D3 (147 Hz) and the A clarinet, which has a lower limit of C3 (139 Hz). The highest fundamental lies around G6 (1.57 kHz). When played softly, notes in the octave above middle C contain frequencies up to 1.5 kHz; when played loudly, the clarinet's spectrum can range up to 12 kHz.

The frequency components of the clarinet radiate exclusively from the finger holes at frequencies between 800 Hz and 3 kHz; but as the pitch rises, more of the sound emanates from the bell (Figure 4-9).

Clarinet Tip

A reflective floor surface reflects the upper frequencies back to the listener, producing a more brilliant sound.

Figure 4-9
Clarinet

1. If the player holds the instrument correctly, the best mic placement is to aim at the lower finger holes at a distance of 6–12" (Mic 1, CD Track 13). In this way, the sounds originating from the finger holes and the bell are picked up with equal intensity.

2. If isolation is needed, to reduce leakage from other instruments, placing a mic or lapel mic near the instrument's bell will produce acceptable results (Mic 2, CD Track 13). Be aware that all the sound doesn't come out of the bell, rather the level of the notes tends to decrease as they move down the scale. For this reason, a standard mic, with a flat frequency response, would provide better results than a clip or lapel mic, which is typically rolled off in the low end. Using a compressor might help even out the note-to-note level differences that are often encountered when miking a woodwind bell (See Chapter 7: *Outboard Stuff*).

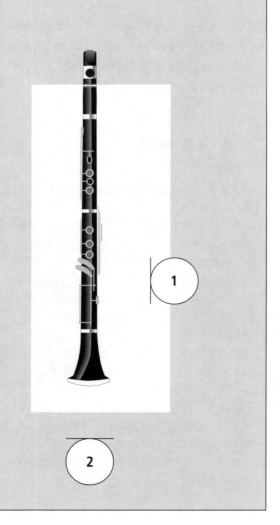

Clavichord

The clavichord is one of the most popular baroque period keyboard instruments, with about four octaves of range. The action consists simply of a piano-type key that's connected via a stick to a brass blade which pivots upward to strike the string when played.

The Clavichord has a small soundboard with a bridge mounted on it over which the strings run. It produces a very quiet, low-level sound, which often makes the mechanical sound of the keys quite noticeable. Because of the very low levels of the instrument, it's often necessary to close-mic it with a high-quality large-diaphragm condenser mic (even in a noise-free environment).

Good results usually can be obtained by placing a mic about 4–6 inches directly above the middle of the bridge over the soundboard, or by placing an X-Y stereo pair in the same position.

A spaced stereo pair placed 4–6 inches to each side of the bridge's midpoint over the soundboard, will also provide good results (see the 3:1 spacing rule in Chapter 3).

Didgeridoo

This Australian aboriginal instrument is enjoying a great deal of popularity in many kinds of music throughout the world today. It essentially consists of a four or five foot pipe, played by blowing into one end—usually with the other end resting on the ground or just a few inches above it. An accurate recording can be made with the mic placed about 12 inches in front of the end.

The digeridoo produces low notes that reverberate around the room; sometimes it's this reverberant sound that's desired. It can be picked up with an omnidirectional room mic that's placed a few feet away and blended in with the close mic. If just the reverberant sound is desired, the didgeridoo can be recorded with an X-Y or Blumlein coincident stereo pair at a distance of 6–12 feet from the player.

Didgeroo Tip

Having the player perform on a reflective floor surface—i.e., by taking up the area rug or putting down a sheet of plywood—will add to the overall reflection of the sound into the mic and/or the room.

Dobro/Resophonic Guitar

The Dobro or resophonic guitar—which is often used in Southern traditional blues and folk music—produces its sound from a metal resonator, and is played in the same way as a regular acoustic guitar. It can also be found in bluegrass bands where it's played horizontally like a steel guitar. The mic techniques in Figure 4-10 are used for bluegrass style playing, with the dobro's front facing up.

Dobro Tips

- For stereo, try a large-diaphragm condenser mic over the treble bout sound hole, and a small-diaphragm condenser mic over the tailpiece end (Figure 4-10, Mics 1 and 4).
- A resophonic guitar that's played like a regular guitar can be miked in much the same way as an acoustic guitar.

Figure 4-10
Dobro

1. The Dobro has a sweet spot, usually over the treble "bout" away from the player, where the small round sound hole or f hole is located. Listen for this spot, and mic the instrument with a condenser mic about 12" above it (Mic 1, CD Track 14).

2. Moving the mic over the center of the resonator gives a less mellow sound with more highs (Mic 2, CD Track 14).

3. Miking over the tailpiece gives more treble and less body (Mic 3, CD Track 14).

4. For a smooth sound that minimizes noise, try a condenser mic about 6" in front of the front edge and about 2" above the top, pointed straight across the top at the spot that sounds best between the bridge and the end of the fingerboard (Mic 4, CD Track 14).

Drum Set

The drum set is usually the backbone of modern recorded music, in that it provides the "heart beat" of the basic rhythm track. Because of this, a proper drum sound is extremely important to the final impact of a recording. Today's drum set is generally made up of a bass (kick) drum, a snare drum, high-tom (one or more), low-tom (one or more), hi-hat and a variety of cymbals. Since a full drum set is a series of interrelated and closely spaced percussion instruments, it's often difficult to attain a proper sense of spatial and tonal balance. To do it right takes patience, practice, and dedication—just ask any pro.

The larger-than-life, driving sound of the acoustic drum set is the result of expert balance between professional playing technique, proper tuning, and proper mic placement. As a general rule, a poorly played or tuned drum will sound just as bad through a good mic as it will through a bad one; thus, it's important that the drum sound good to the ears before you begin to critically place the mics.

Miking the Drum Set

Once the drum set has been tuned and adjusted for the best sound, the microphones can be positioned. Although the drum set needs to be viewed as a single entity, from a practical point of view, and since each part of the set is so different in sound and function, we'll be considering each as an individual instrument and will mic them accordingly. The characteristics that assist in this match-up include frequency response, polar response, proximity effect, and transient response. The dynamic range of a microphone and its ability to handle high levels are also important characteristics to consider when miking a drum set. The set is capable of generating extreme volume and power as well as soft, subtle sounds that add color to the music. The peak SPL of a drum kit can range to over 150 dB for the kick, toms and cymbals. A mic and the console's input preamps must be able to withstand these peaks without distorting, and they must be able to capture each nuance without adding noise.

Drum Set Tips

- As the drum set is usually one of the loudest sound sources in the sound studio, the drum set is often placed on a 1–1 1/2 foot high riser, in order to reduce bass leakage. In preventing drum leakage to other mics, four foot flats are often placed around the drum set.

- It almost goes without saying that the acoustic drum set can be a leakage nightmare. If you run into severe leakage problems, you might want to consider placing the drums in an isolation booth or room—hopefully one with a window so the drummer can see what's going on.

- You might want to minimize room reverberation through the use of gobos, blankets, mattresses, or other sound absorbing material. Unwanted room sound can interfere with getting a clean drum sound.

- If you want a bigger-than-life sound, reserve the largest studio room for the drums and isolate everyone else via direct boxes, overdubs and/or separate rooms. The large room size will add to the drum's impact and let you place a distant spaced stereo pair out into the room. To this, all we can add is: Have fun and experiment!

Kick Drum (Bass Drum)

Low-frequency reproduction at high sound pressure levels is essential to the quality pickup of a kick drum. For this reason, mics that are designed to reproduce low-frequency signals at high working levels are often chosen. This typically means choosing a large diaphragm dynamic microphone such as the AKG D-12E or D112, Electro-Voice N/D868 or RE20, Shure Beta 56, Sennheiser E602, Audio-Technica ATM25, or the Beyer TGX-50.

You'll probably want to experiment with the player's kick since each one has it's own special character. Because of the instrument's design and the extreme proximity effect that's encountered at close working distances, even a minor change in placement can have a profound effect on the pickup (Figure 4-11).

Kick Drum Tips

- Placing a blanket or other damping material inside the drum shell, firmly against the beater head, tightens a dull and loose kick sound to a sharper, more defined, transient sound. Padding in front of the drum also helps give more definition.

- Cutting the kick's equalization at 300–600 Hz reduces the dull, cardboard sound while

Figure 4-11
Kick Drum (Bass Drum)

1. A microphone placement close to the beater picks up a hard beater sound (Mic 1, CD Track 15).

2. An off-center placement (Mic 2, CD Track 15) will pick up more of a skin tone.

3. Moving the microphone closer to the head inside the drum adds warmth and fullness, while moving it farther back often emphasizes the high-frequency click (Mic 3, CD Track 15).

4. If the rear head of the drum is on, placing the mic near the center of the rear head will produce a boomier, less defined sound when close-miked (Mic 4, CD Track 15).

5. Miking the rear head off center may reduce some of this boominess; however, it will often pick up more of the head's skin tone (Mic 5, CD Track 15).

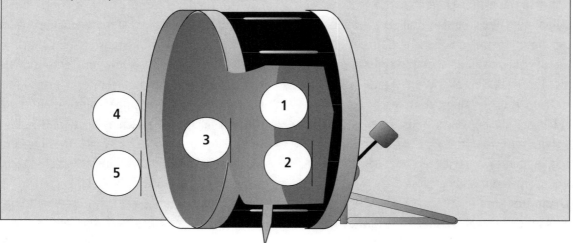

boosting from 2.5–5 kHz provides a sharper attack, adding an enhanced click or snap to the sound.

Snare Drum

When miking the snare drum, a compromise is needed between the ideal microphone placement and the movements of the drummer. Therefore, one of the first considerations is simply that of finding a safe place for the microphone—a position where it won't be bashed in by a passing stick (Figure 4-12).

Hi-hat

The sound of the hi-hat falls within the same overall frequency range as the snare drum, but the hi-hat produces a lot more high-frequency energy. In contrast, the snare's sound is concentrated in the midrange (Figure 4-13).

Hi-hat Tips

• Moving the hi-hat microphone doesn't change the overall sound as much as it does on the snare.

• The opening and closing motion of the hi-hat produces rushes of air; therefore, the mic shouldn't be placed directly off the cymbal edges.

High Toms

The high (rack) toms can be miked either individually or with a single overall microphone placed a short distance between the two toms (Figure 4-14).

Figure 4-12
Snare drum

1. For rock drumming, a cardioid mic is generally aimed just inside the top rim of the snare drum, at a distance of about 1" (Mic 1, CD Track 16). The mic should be aimed away from the other drums and cymbals for the best separation. A hypercardioid pattern can be used to reduce leakage from other drums. Its rejection angle can be aimed at either the hi-hat or high toms (depending on leakage difficulties). Dynamic mics, such as the Shure SM57, are often used on snare drums, although small-diaphragm condensers typically give a tight, present sound.

2. In certain musical forms, such as jazz, a crisp sound may be desired. Facing a mic at the bottom head (Mic 2, CD Track 16), in addition to the mic for the top head can do this. Since the bottom head is 180° out of phase with the top, it's wise to reverse the phase polarity of this mic.

3. A clip or lapel mic can also be suspended from the snare's rim aimed just inside the top rim of the snare drum, at a distance of about 1" (Mic 3, CD Track 16).

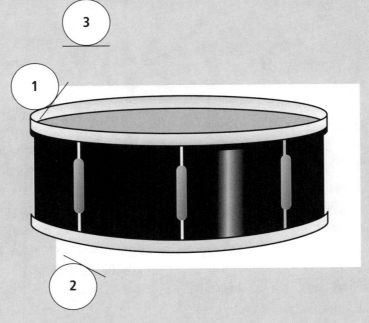

Figure 4-13
Hi-hat

1. Placing the mic over the edge of the top cymbal (Mic 1, CD Track 17) usually produces the brightest sound. Placing the mic above the top cymbal reproduces all the nuances of stick attack. Angling the mic toward the edge of the cymbal and away from the drummer helps keep other drums out of the mix.

2. A single mic can be used for both the snare and hi-hat by placing it equidistant between the two (Mic 2, CD Track 17) and facing it away from the high-toms (a bidirectional mic pointed towards the two works great).

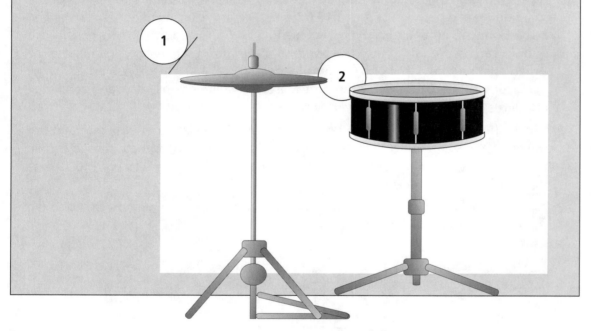

Low Tom

The recommended mic placement for the low tom is similar to that for the high tom: about 1–3 inches above the top head. Again, one microphone can be used between two low toms, but one mic per drum gives greater control over panning and tonal color (CD Track 19).

Cymbals

Cymbals can be miked in a variety of ways. Although there are no rules, the method you chose will tend to depend on the style of music being recorded. For example, if you're recording rock, you might want to get the immediacy that comes from individually miking each cymbal; if you're recording lite rock or jazz, you might want to use a stereo overhead pair; if you're short on mics or want to be inventive, you could use a single mic over the set or use distant-miking techniques to create a sense of space (Figure 4-15).

Individual Miking

This technique is often used in rock music—when gazillions of tracks are available—because it provides an immediate sound that can be easily controlled.

Try a small diaphragm condenser microphone about 6–8 inches above the side of each cymbal opposite where the stick hits (Figure 4-15, Mic 1, CD Track 20).

Place a cardioid condenser or stereo mic 2–3 feet above the cymbals on each side of the set, positioned to pick up the cymbals equally (Figure 4-15, Mics 2, CD Track 20).

Overhead Miking

This technique generally involves two mics placed over the drum kit to pickup the high-frequency transients of cymbals with crisp accurate detail while providing an overall blend of the entire drum set. Because of these transients,

Figure 4-14
High-Toms

1. When miked individually (Mic Setup 1, CD Track 18), the microphone can be placed close to the top head (about 1" over and 2" in from the rim). This will give a tight, "dead" sound that has less shell resonance and more head attack. This distance can be increased to about 3" in order to give a more live sound.

2. A single microphone can be used on two high-toms (Mic 2, CD Track 18) by placing it between and slightly above the drums. To reduce overall leakage or feedback potential, a hypercardioid pattern can be chosen.

To get a big, boom-like "thud" sound, to reduce leakage, and to get the pickup out of the drummer's way, remove the bottom heads from the toms and mic them inside, a few inches away from the head. The sound picked up from inside the tom will generally yield less of an attack and have a fuller tone.

Figure 4-15
Cymbals

"Cymbals can be miked in a variety of ways. Although there are no rules, the method that you chose will tend to depend on the style of music that's being recorded."

a small-diaphragm condenser microphone is often chosen for its accurate high-end response. While the choice of overhead mic positioning is quite subjective, two popular methods dominate: 3:1 positioning and coincident positioning.

When using an overhead pair in a 3:1 spacing position (Figure 4-15, Mic Setup 3, CD Track 20), the widest stereo image is obtained by spacing the matched mics over the set with the mics facing slightly away from each other in an outward fashion. Phasing problems may occur as a result of sound waves arriving at each pickup point at differing times.

If the 3:1 rule doesn't fix this problem to your satisfaction, try positioning the mics in a closely spaced X-Y coincident array (Figure 4-15, Stereo Mic Setup 4, CD Track 20). In this way, a stereo image is maintained and—as there's little distance between microphones—all sounds arrive in phase at both microphones. This prevents phase cancellations whenever the recording is heard in mono. (See Chapter 6: *Stereo Miking Techniques* for a more detailed description of 3:1 spacing and coincident stereo techniques.)

Important Overhead Miking Tip

With certain drum miking setups, the need for separate overhead microphones may be reduced or entirely eliminated. This is due to the leakage from the cymbals into the snare and tom mics. In addition, in a live reinforcement situation the loud cymbals may be easily heard above the overall pickup.

Minimal Miking

Although drum kits are often recorded by individually miking most or all drums, you might run into a situation where you have to use fewer mics.

It's not a crime to use several mics to pick

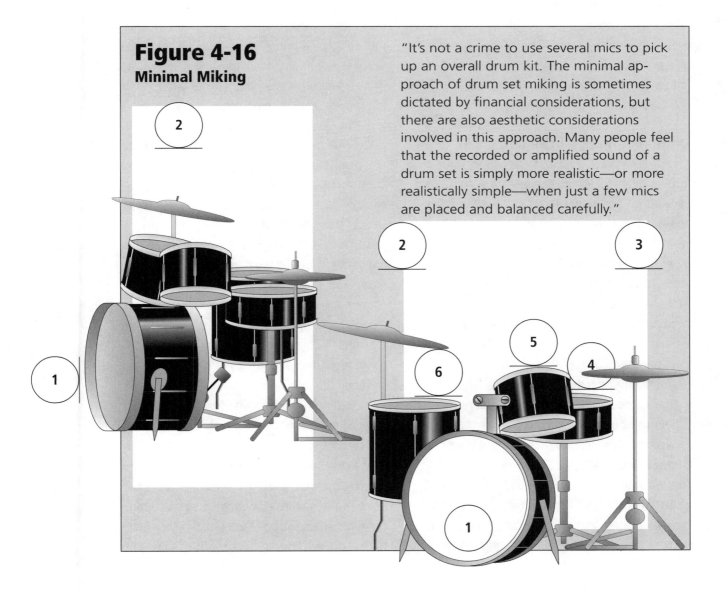

Figure 4-16
Minimal Miking

"It's not a crime to use several mics to pick up an overall drum kit. The minimal approach of drum set miking is sometimes dictated by financial considerations, but there are also aesthetic considerations involved in this approach. Many people feel that the recorded or amplified sound of a drum set is simply more realistic—or more realistically simple—when just a few mics are placed and balanced carefully."

up an overall drum kit. The minimal approach of drum set miking is sometimes dictated by financial considerations, but there are also aesthetic considerations involved in this approach. Many people feel that the recorded or amplified sound of a drum set is simply more realistic—or more realistically simple—when just a few mics are placed and balanced carefully. This is often true in recording jazz and country drumming. For a minimal setup that combines individual control over key elements with a balanced pickup of the whole set, place a quality dynamic or condenser microphone between the snare and hi-hat, an extended bottom-range mic at the bass drum, and a quality condenser overhead. If stereo imaging is important, use an overhead pair (CD Track 21).

Distant-Miking of the Drum Set

When "new music" came on the scene, distant-miking techniques in the recording studio became an additional tool to getting a fuller more ambient sound. Such distant techniques, which may be used in addition to or in place of traditional close-miking techniques, often use the following approaches:

- Place a spaced microphone pair 10–20 feet from the set, facing toward the source.
- Place a coincident (X-Y or Blumlein) microphone pair 10–20 feet from the set, facing toward the source.
- Place a boundary (i.e., PZM) mic pair 10–20 feet in front of the set, on the floor, on the walls or anywhere you want to put them.

Distant Drum Miking Tip

This technique relies heavily upon the acoustics of a studio or room, which affect the recorded sound. For best results when only one sound source is being recorded, use an omnidirectional or boundary microphone.

Hand Drums

There are many types of hand drums found throughout the world. Most have a body that's somewhat longer than the diameter of the head, and are made to be played under the arm with a strap or across the lap—when sitting down or resting on the ground. Some have cylindrical shaped bodies while others have bodies with necks down the center that flare out at the bottom to form a port. The waisted or hourglass types are shaped somewhat like a wineglass goblet, and others are shaped like barrels that may have a head at each end.

These types of drums are among the earliest musical instruments known, so they have had many centuries to develop into different shapes, sizes, and uses. They can produce many different sounds depending on how and where they're struck, and whether the sound comes from the head, body, or a combination of the head and the bottom port. The unique sound of many hourglass drums comes as much from the rear port as from the head. Often the head produces the sharp sound of the strike while a deep boom emanates from the other end. The combinations of these sounds are employed by the musician to shape the music.

It's often much more difficult to properly record the sounds that emanate from the rear of the drum, since room resonance is commonly an integral part of the sound. Your best bet is to listen to the instrument for awhile to get familiar with the sound, talking with the performer or producer about the characteristics they want to hear on the recording. Walk around the room;

Figure 4-17
Hand drum

- As much of the distinctive sound comes from the rear port of a tapered-body hand drum, try miking the front as per Mic 1, and also mic the rear port with a condenser mic at a distance of 6"–2'. Blend the two or mix them to stereo (Mic 2, CD Track 22). Reverse the phase on the rear mic.

- When overdubbing or when leakage isn't a problem, use a good condenser mic at a greater distance (2–6') to allow the instrument to "breath" and to pick up its sweet spot (Mic 3, CD Track 22). This may take several trial recordings with different mic placements to hone in on the desired sound.

- Sometimes, great sounds are free for the pickin' by placing a spaced, X-Y or Blumlein stereo pair out in the middle of the room (either facing toward or away from the player).

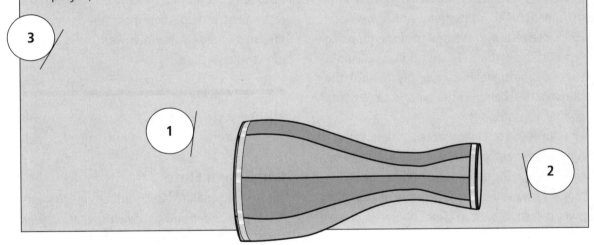

have the performer try different places in the room to find the place or places where you can hear the desired sound.

The sound from the head is relatively easy to record using basically the same techniques that are used on a snare or tom. Simply place a dynamic or condenser a few inches above the head, off to one side and angled toward the head (Mic 1, CD Track 22). Feel free to move the mic a few inches closer to or farther from the head, adjusting the angle until you get the head sound you (and the musician) want (Figure 4-17).

Hand Drum Tip

Always check phase between the close and the room mic by listening to both channels mixed in monaural. If bringing up the room mic decreases the boom, try changing its phase.

Dulcimer

Hammer Dulcimer
The hammer dulcimer is a trapezoidal instrument that has several courses of strings stretched across the soundboard, over a bridge at one side

and under the bridge at the other side. The strings are struck with small wooden hammers. The low strings are at the bottom of the instrument and the scale runs up to the top. Commonly, these lilting bell-like instruments measure out at about three feet wide at the bottom, tapering to about two feet at the top. They can either be placed on a table or can be mounted on a floor-stand that's tilted toward the player.

A hammer dulcimer can be miked with a single mic (preferably a large-diaphragm cardioid condenser) above the outer rim of the instrument at about 12–24 inches—depending upon room acoustics and potential leakage from other instruments. This placement works well and won't interfere with the ability of the player to hammer the strings. In addition, you might want to point the mic inwardly toward the soundboard—being a little off axis can smooth the highest notes out.

An X-Y coincident stereo pickup (at the same placement point) can give you a great stereo image. The pan positioning can be varied from very wide for a solo instrument to a narrower pan for a backup (See Chapter 6: *Stereo Miking*).

Mountain Dulcimer

The Mountain Dulcimer is an instrument that's about three feet long and 6–8 inches wide— usually with three strings running the entire length over a fretboard. It's generally played on one's lap and is strummed with a quill pick or the fingers. This type of dulcimer produces a fairly soft sound and can have a fair amount of pick noise up close.

If pick noise and harshness aren't a problem, place a high-quality condenser or ribbon mic above and to the side of the instrument—off axis at a distance of 1–2 feet.

While the sound radiates from the top, to minimize pick noise and harshness you can aim a high-quality condenser or ribbon mic at the player's chest, above the level of the instrument, thereby making use of the mic's off-axis pickup response.

The above positions also work for coincident stereo miking (See Chapter 6: *Stereo Miking*). If the player also sings, the same mic can be adjusted to pick up the vocal. If the performer's vocal is to be picked up by a separate vocal mic, use a cardioid mic for the vocal and point it up at an angle to minimize instrument pickup, then move the instrument mic to the side and downward to minimize direct voice pickup.

flute

End-Blown Flute

The end-blown flute family includes instruments like the recorder and pennywhistle, as well as flutes like the Japanese Shakuhachi. In all of these cases, the sound comes both from the mouthpiece and the lowest open finger hole. Some of these flutes are soft and low-pitched while others are quite loud and high-pitched. For example, a C pennywhistle sounds shrill and loud; whereas, a C recorder sounds mellow and much softer.

As all of these instruments operate on the same principal—the mic techniques are basically the same. The chosen recording technique and the mic distance from the instrument will often depend as much on how much room sound is desired as anything else. Since the sound emanates mostly from the lowest open hole, for close-miking position the mic at about six inches over the body of the instrument, midway between the head and the end.

If more room resonance is desired, the mic can be moved farther away. Recorders in classical music can be treated like a transverse flute and miked from a greater distance. Often recorders are played in ensemble and many baroque works have been written for recorder trios and quartets. These ensembles can be effectively miked with a coincident stereo microphone setup positioned to give the proper balance between the instruments.

Figure 4-18
Transverse Flute

- For contemporary pop music, mic distance can range from 1–2' (Mic 1, CD Track 23).

- For classical and solo playing, try placing the microphone on axis and slightly above the player at a distance of 3–8' (Mic 2, CD Track 23).

- Placing the mic directly in front of the mouthpiece might be desirable in a high-feedback, high-leakage environment, although this placement greatly accentuates breath noises. To minimize breath noise in this type of close-mic technique, position the mic 2–6" above the player, pointing it down towards the mouthpiece, so the breath blows past and beneath the mic (Mic 3, CD Track 23).

- If the acoustic environment is so extreme that a mic distance of 3/4–2" in front of the mouthpiece is needed, you should instruct the player to blow below the microphone to reduce air stream noises and blasts.

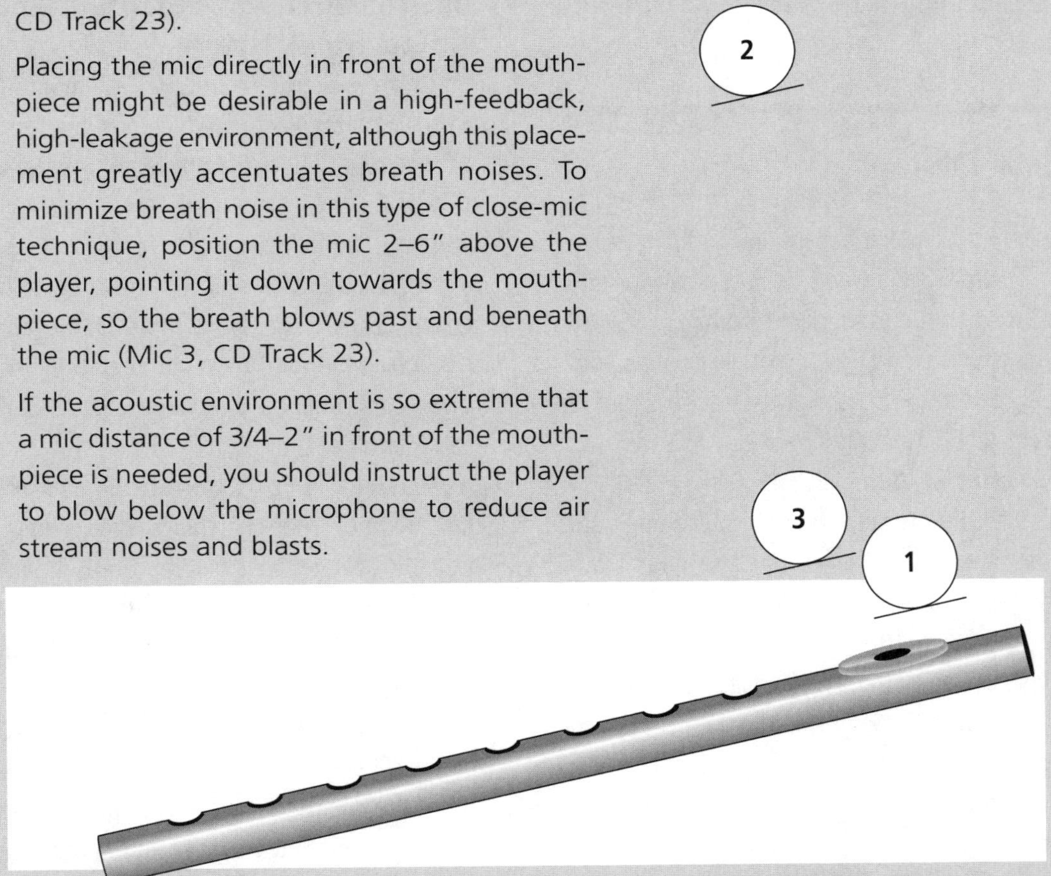

Transverse Flute

The fundamental range of the flute extends from about B3 to C7 (247 Hz to 2.1 kHz). For medium-loud tones, the upper overtone limit lies between 3 and 6 kHz. At frequencies up to 3 kHz, the instrument's sound is radiated along the flautist's line-of-sight; above this point the direction of radiation swings to about 90° to the right of the player. The sound comes from both the mouthpiece as well as the first open finger hole. In most circumstances, a microphone should be positioned midway between the mouthpiece and bell. In this manner, both the characteristic breath sound and tone quality will be picked up with equal intensity. Microphone placement often depends upon the type of music being played and room acoustics (Figure 4-18).

French Horn

The French horn is a notoriously difficult instrument to play with a clean intonation and sound. Its fundamentals range from Bl to B5 (65–700 Hz). Its round broad quality comes from an "oo" sound, or formant that can be found at about 340 Hz, while others fall between 750 Hz and 2 kHz, as well as around 3.5 kHz.

French horn players often place one hand inside the bell, which mutes the sound and promotes a formant at about 3 kHz. Frequencies from 62 to 100 Hz radiate uniformly from the instrument. With rising frequencies, however, this angle trims down to within 15° of off axis.

For the above reason, place a mic behind the player at a distance of 1–4 feet, facing into the bell at a slightly off-axis angle.

Traditionally, the French horn player or section is placed at the rear of an ensemble, just in front of a rear reflective stage wall. Because of its curvature, the bell faces the wall, which reflects the sound back toward the listener's position, creating a fuller, more defined French horn sound. An effective pickup can be had by using a bidirectional mic on axis to the horn, in order to receive both the direct and reflected sound; or the mic can be placed in front of the horn section, on axis to the reflective surface, so that only the reflected sound is picked up.

Acoustic Guitar

Flat-top, Arch Top, Plectrum, Finger Picked, Steel, Nylon

There are several techniques for miking the acoustic guitar, each of which produces its own distinct sound; likewise, there are several types of guitars that also have their own special character and application. Major differences among guitars include (1) flat-top or arch top design, (2) nylon or steel strings, (3) played with a plectrum, finger picks or just the fingers, (4) chord strummed or lead picked, (5) backup, lead instrument, or both.

Guitars can be subtle instruments, requiring care in microphone choice and technique in order to get the best results. The instrument's body shape, type of strings, and the player's style all effect the tone, and influence both placement and technique (Figure 4-19).

Microphone placement varies from instrument to instrument, requiring experimentation to get the desired sound. A change in mic positioning—sometimes by just a small amount—affects the tone, attack pickup, brightness,

Figure 4-19
Acoustic guitar

"Room acoustics also play a large role in acoustic guitar recording. Some people find that acoustically dead rooms give them the sound they want while others prefer small rooms with lots of reverb. The most natural sound generally can be achieved in a controlled acoustic environment with some reverberation and some dead spots. Moving the guitarist around in such a room can make a dramatic difference in the recorded sound."

boominess, balance, and pick and finger noise pickup. The guitar radiates sound from its entire body; so, the closer the mic, the more the recording will accentuate the sound that's coming from just one portion of the instrument. Before setting up the mic, listen to the guitar, moving your ear to different places and at different distances, until you find the place that appears to give you the sound you want. Try placing a large or small diaphragm condenser mic there as an initial start point. Beyond this, here are some basic guidelines:

• Try pointing the mic towards the body end of the fingerboard from a distance of six inches to two feet (Figure 4-19, Mic 1, CD Track 24). Typically, this produces the most balanced sound with good overtones from a flat-top

guitar and is one of the first mic positions to try. The tonal balance can be adjusted by moving or pointing the mic toward the soundhole, if more bass is desired, and away from the soundhole if you want less bass. If noise from sliding fingers on the strings is a problem, try angling the mic more toward the soundhole.

• Miking directly above the bridge from 8–18 inches picks up a lot of harmonic overtones, but can also accentuate pick noise (Figure 4-19, Mic 2, CD Track 24). This is a good place to start miking a nylon string guitar that's played with the fingers. Placing the mic over the bridge while aiming it at the soundhole will slightly accentuate the bass.

• A mic technique that's not too common, but

is effective in producing a balanced sound, with a minimum of bass boom and pick and finger noise, utilizes a large-diaphragm condenser mic horizontal with the floor, with the diaphragm pointing up (Figure 4-19, Mic 3, CD Track 24). The player sits down and positions the mic under the widest part of the guitar, so the diaphragm is just peeking over the top (like a setting sun just touching the horizon), pointing directly across the top behind the bridge. The guitar shouldn't touch the mic and the player should avoid moving the guitar. Very good results can be obtained, when a guitarist understands this technique and can work with it.

- The sound hole on the front of a guitar serves as a bass port that resonates at lower frequencies (around 80–100 Hz). A microphone placed too close to this port tends to sound boomy and unnatural. This is, however, a popular miking position on stage or around high acoustic levels because the guitar's output is highest at this point (Figure 4-19, Mic 4, CD Track 24). To achieve a more natural pickup under these conditions, the microphone's output can be rolled off at the lower frequencies (5–10 dB at 100 Hz). The closer the mic is to the soundhole, the more boom will be recorded. In addition, as the mic gets closer the sound definition from higher overtones decreases. This position also picks up a great deal of pick noise. A cardioid mic positioned above the soundhole while pointing toward the end of the fingerboard still picks up the boom—and at the same time moves the high-frequency pick noise off axis.

- Miking behind the bridge (Figure 4-19, Mic 5, CD Track 24) reduces bass boom, accentuates the midrange some and produces a clean woody sound with lots of subharmonics. Using your ears, you can usually find a sweet spot near this point. It's usually not right behind the center of the bridge, but more toward the treble side, a few inches over the instrument.

- Sometimes two or more mics are blended together to capture the best recording. Some engineers mic the back of the guitar as well as the front (Figure 4-19, Mic Setup 6— Mics 1 and 6, CD Track 24), with the rear mic being placed out-of-phase with the front to pick up more bass. Others choose a close mic for presence pickup and a more distant mic for ambience. If more than one mic is used, check for possible phase problems by bringing one mic up to listening level, slowly raising the level of the second mic and listening in mono for a decrease in volume or softening of the sound.

- Solo or lead guitars often are recorded in stereo, generally using a coincident stereo miking technique. However a spaced pair configuration (Figure 4-19, Mic Setup 7— Mics 1 and 5, CD Track 24) can be used with one mic above the end of the fingerboard and the other behind the bridge (see Chapter 6: *Stereo Miking*).

Pickups are widely used in acoustic guitars, effectively turning them into a type of electric guitar. Pickups typically don't produce the same sound as a miked instrument but can give you a full Les Paul or Chet Atkins sound that can really hit the spot. If the pickup sound is all that you want, the instrument can be treated as an electric guitar and recorded using the same techniques. Most often, however, the pickup is run into the board using a DI and is blended with the miked acoustic sound.

Acoustic Guitar Tip

Room acoustics also play a large role in acoustic guitar recording. Some people find that acoustically dead rooms give them the sound they want while others prefer small rooms with lots of reverb. The most natural sound generally can be achieved in a controlled acoustic environment with some reverberation and some dead spots. Moving the guitarist around in such a room can make a dramatic difference in the recorded sound.

Classical Guitar

The small bodied classical guitar is normally strung with nylon or gut, and is played with the fingertips, giving it a warm, mellow sound that has few of the higher overtones produced by the steel string acoustic.

By placing the microphone over the point near the center of the bridge, at a distance of between 8 and 18 inches, you can pick up the instrument's upper harmonics. At this point the overtones are at their loudest and are reinforced by the guitar's top face.

Classical Guitar Tip

When miking a classical instrument under solo conditions, a greater working distance might be desirable.

Arch Top Guitar

The arch top guitar—widely used in jazz and swing styles—has f holes that work in much the same way as an acoustic's round soundhole.

These guitars have a considerable "snap" and "bark" that's full of mid and treble overtones. These overtones provide punch when used for rhythm playing. Arch top guitars also have a lot of projection, which is why they can be heard along with all the horns, drums and other instruments of the big band, for which they were developed.

Placing the mic a 4–6 inches above the treble side f hole produces good results. For rhythm playing, try backing the mic off to 1 1/2 feet or more.

Electric Guitar

The fundamentals of the average 22 fret guitar extend from E2 to D6 (82 Hz to 1.7 kHz), with overtones pushing this upper range much higher. Not all of these frequencies are necessarily amplified, as the electric guitar cord tends to attenuate frequencies above 5 kHz—unless the guitar has a built-in low-impedance converter. The frequency limitations of the average guitar loudspeaker often add to this effect: it has an upper limit of 5–6 kHz.

The electric guitar can be recorded in a number of ways:

- By placing a mic in front of the amp's loudspeaker
- By plugging a direct box (DI) into the guitar, or the amplifier's external speaker jack
- By recording it using both a mic and direct box.
- For a good pickup with a high degree of separation, a mic can be placed at a distance of two inches to one foot (Figure 4-20, Mic 1, CD Track 25). A clean amp can sound good miked as far as four feet away.
- When miking at a distance of less than six inches, microphone and speaker placement becomes slightly more critical. For a brighter sound, the mic should face directly into the center of the speaker's cone—right where the center starts to flare out (Figure 4-20, Mic 2, CD Track 25). This usually produces the sweetest tone. Placing the microphone off center

to the cone produces a mellower sound while reducing amplifier noise (Figure 4-20, Mic 3, CD Track 25). In addition, angling the mic so the sound pickup is somewhat off axis can result in a darker tone.

- A second, wide-range condenser mic can be used on the same or different speaker and

blended with the dynamic to extend high and low frequencies. For fatter sound during an overdub, try a miking the speaker close with one mic and about 6–8 feet away with another, blending them together (Figure 4-20, Mic Setup 4—Mics 3 and 4, CD Track 25). You might want to try a dynamic for the close

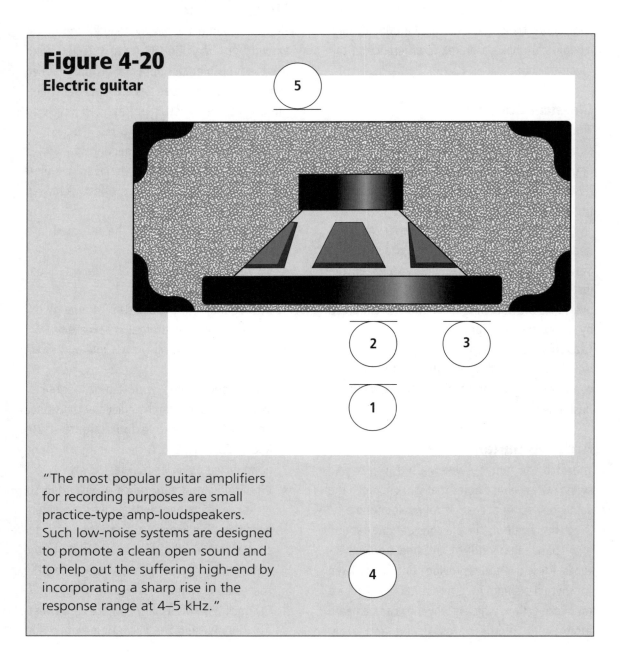

Figure 4-20
Electric guitar

"The most popular guitar amplifiers for recording purposes are small practice-type amp-loudspeakers. Such low-noise systems are designed to promote a clean open sound and to help out the suffering high-end by incorporating a sharp rise in the response range at 4–5 kHz."

mic and a wide-range, large-diaphragm condenser for the other.

- Another method is to use an amp with an open back, miking both the front and the back of the cabinet (Figure 4-20, Mic Setup 5— Mics 3 and 5, CD Track 25). Be sure to check for mono phase compatibility, as you'll probably want to reverse the phase of the rear mic. Amplifier levels should be at a normal playing volume. Have fun experimenting!

- For a clean sound, consider using a DI. Use a short low capacitance cable to avoid cable coloration due to the guitar's relatively high output impedance. Like the above two mic schemes, a DI can also be blended with an amplifier mic (Figure 4-20, Mic 1, 2 or 3 and DI).

- If a multi-speaker cabinet is being miked, two speakers can be miked, with a mic pointed at the center of one speaker and a mic at the edge of the other (Figure 4-20, Mics 1 and 3). In a four-speaker cabinet, the top speakers often have more treble and the bottom more bass. Listen first to determine which speakers to mic: often there are variations in sound from one speaker to the next, even in the same cabinet.

The most popular guitar amplifiers for recording purposes are small practice-type amp-loudspeakers. Such low-noise systems are designed to promote a clean open sound and to help out the suffering high-end by incorporating a sharp rise in the response range at 4–5 kHz. The most popular type of microphone used for the electric guitar cabinet is the cardioid dynamic microphone (like the Shure SM57 or 58), because it adds a full-bodied character to the sound without picking up extraneous amplifier noises. This type of mic has a presence peak in the upper-frequency range that gives an added clarity to the sound. The cardioid pattern is chosen to reduce leakage. Having said all this, don't be afraid to experiment around with either a condenser or ribbon microphone; some great results can be attained with them as well.

Amplified Guitar Tip

When miking at a distance of greater than six inches, phase effects due to boundary interference with the floor can be reduced by placing the cabinet on top of a chair, or by laying a small amount of carpet on the floor.

Harmonica

While harmonicas (harps) come in many shapes, sizes and keys, they're divided into two basic types: diatonic and chromatic. The length, width and thickness of the vibrating reed determines the pitch, while the harp player's habit of forming his or her hands around the instrument molds the tone by forming a resonant cavity.

As part of their technique, harp players like to get close to the microphone, deepening the tone or getting a special "washing" effect by opening and closing one hand. Often, they hold the microphone in the cavity formed by their palms. For this reason, harmonica players often carry a preferred microphone with them, rather than get stuck in front of an unfamiliar microphone and stand. Especially for blues harmonica players, the Shure 520D Green Bullet microphone has become an integral part of their sound.

If the player has their own mic, they'll know exactly how to get the sound they want. Otherwise, the harmonica is usually miked quite closely using a good quality dynamic or condenser mic with a very good windscreen that can handle the breath blasts. A little compression might be necessary to even out the sound.

Harp

Two kinds of harps are commonly encountered today: the full sized orchestral harp and the considerably smaller folk or Irish harp. The harp's sound radiates from the soundboard that runs diagonally up from the bottom. The strings are attached to this soundboard; thus, the sound emanates from a fairly large surface (Figure 4-21).

Harpsichord

The harpsichord is a keyboard instrument similar to, but smaller than, a piano. However, the major difference is that the harpsichord

Figure 4-21
Harp

- Positioning the mic close to the soundboard, at any given point along it, will only emphasize the sounds that radiate from that particular surface. However, if a particular range of the scale is desired (in a nonclassical recording session), a mic can be placed at the desired point, from a distance of 6"–1' (Mic 1, CD Track 26). A few test recordings with different close-miked positions will identify the proper placement.

- For a more natural, classical sound, it's necessary to move the mic 2' or more from a full sized harp (Mic 2, CD Track 26), and 1' or more from an Irish harp. A good starting position is about level with the player's hands, pointing at the soundboard. Try a large-diaphragm, flat-response condenser mic. For those wanting to record in stereo, try a co-incident pair in the same location you would use for a single mic (Mic 2), or try placing two mics at a compromise point between the strings and the soundboard at the upper and lower ranges of the instrument (Mics 3).

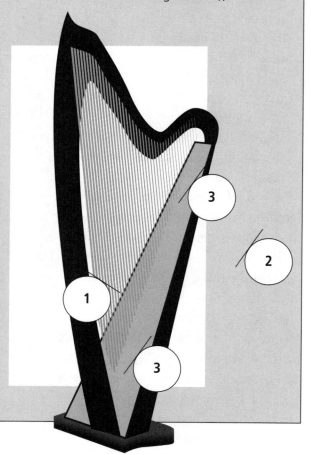

strings are plucked by a quill instead of being struck by a hammer. A single strung harpsichord is generally a very soft instrument; those that have more than one string per note can be substantially louder.

All the techniques mentioned for miking a grand piano could be tried on the harpsichord.

Although the sound output can be low, the key and jack mechanism of a harpsichord produces a fair amount of noise. While greater presence can be achieved by close-miking, the noisy action can often be a problem. For the most natural sound, in a very quiet environment, place a coincident stereo pair far enough away to minimize the instrument's action noise while being close enough to get adequate levels.

Horn Section

The horn section in a band can be composed of trumpets, coronets, trombones, saxophones, clarinets and other wind blown instruments. The techniques for individually miking each of these instruments can be found under the listing for that instrument. However, when recording a horn section—part of many funk, R&B, blues, pop, dance, and jazz recordings—the entire section must generally be recorded at the same time, rather than recording each part separately. The players often work together and cue off of one another in a way that can't be captured by separating the instruments or via overdubbing (Figure 4-22).

It might be necessary to use gobos or other sound control to minimize leakage and control

Figure 4-22
Horn section

Horn sections are usually grouped by instrument: trumpets, trombones, saxes, etc. In the studio, these groupings can be separated into seated rows, with cardioid mics positioned in front of 2–4 instruments. Mics are typically placed at a distance where they naturally pick up each instrument in the section (often 3–4'), while minimizing the pickup of other sections (Mic 1).

reverberation. The dispersion pattern of all horns is fairly narrow, so make sure they are positioned within the pattern of the mic. Trombones and saxophones should be grouped as closely together and miked as closely as possible. It also usually doesn't make much difference if the sectional instruments are a little off-axis to the microphone. Mic as close to the bells as you can while keeping the instrument blend in mind; though, don't forget to give the players adequate room to play.

Another popular technique that can be used during an overdub is to group the entire horn section around a single mic or coincident pair that's placed in the center of the room. This can either be a single large-diaphragm condenser in the omni position or it can be two bidirectional pickups, placed in a Blumlein stereo pickup configuration. Group the players around the mic at a distance that's comfortable for them and is appropriate for the amount of room sound and reverberation you'd like to pick up. This technique requires that you carefully blend the instruments acoustically, since you won't be able to fix it in the mix. Take your time! You might want to have the section leader or conductor help you acoustically balance the instruments by having each player move in or out, play softer, play louder, etc. Remember, if this is your technique of choice, you won't have a second chance—unless you want to gather the forces back together again for another session.

Horn Tip

Horns make a lot of sound, so it is essential to not only have a room that's well treated acoustically (to minimize reverberation) but is also large enough to accommodate the section, while letting the sound of the horns blossom out. Not all the players in a horn section produce the same volume, nor necessarily the same emphasis desired in the blend. It is essential that the players position themselves in relation to the microphone to get the blend desired for the section.

Important Tip

If necessary, use a mic pad to prevent overload. Trumpets are quite loud and may need to back off from the mic more than other instruments in the section.

Hurdy Gurdy

The hurdy gurdy has been around since medieval times and is still used today in folk and ethnic bands. Its sound somewhat resembles a droning fiddle, except that the sound is made by cranking a rosin coated wheel that rubs strings, which are stopped or sounded by pressing the keys on a simplified keyboard. This instrument is usually played sitting down with the instrument on the lap facing up. For miking, you can basically treat it like a violin.

Mandolin Family

The mandolin family today encompasses the mandolin, mandola, mando-cello and mando-bass. These instruments are presently used in classical, folk, bluegrass, Celtic and rock/pop music (Figure 4-23).

The mandolin has developed into several types, each of which has its own acoustic properties and musical uses. The older style with a bowl-shaped back and flat top, bent at the bridge to angle down toward the tailpiece at the bridge, is known as the Neapolitan Mandolin. It has a round soundhole and produces a somewhat tinkly sound that's generally softer than other mandolins. Like all mandolins, there's a sharp transient at the moment the string is picked, after which the sound falls off rapidly.

The mandolin most often used in bluegrass is modeled after the Gibson F-5 that was developed in the 1920s, and is easily recognized by its curl and points. This instrument can be quite loud, with a highly percussive attack, especially during chording.

There can be great level variations from lead playing to backup chording, especially on F-5 type mandolins. If this is a problem, have the player either back away from the mic or turn sideways to it for chording. Good chord pickup from an F-5 mandolin in a bluegrass band can be achieved at a miking distance of 2–4 feet while adequate pickup of lead playing may require being only 6–8 inches away from the mic. Sometimes two mics are used to mic an f hole mandolin: one in front of the f hole and one a few inches over the fingerboard where it joins the body. As usual with two-mic techniques, watch for phase problems.

Mandolin Tip

While the mandola and mando-cello can be treated much like a traditional mandolin, the mando-bass (a great big mandolin that's tuned like a bass) shares some of the same problems that are associated with recording the acoustic bass.

Figure 4-23
Mandolin

You can use a small- or large-diaphragm condenser mic when recording a mandolin. For round hole models, try placing the mic 6–18" in front of the sound hole (Mic 1, CD Track 27). For f hole models, place the mic 6–18" in front of the lower f hole (Mic 2, CD Track 27). Greater mic distances reduce pick noise and provide a more balanced sound.

Oboe

This member of the woodwind family makes its sound by blowing on a double reed that's clenched in the lips, causing the column of air to vibrate within its body. Most of the sound of the oboe radiates from the body, rather than the reed or bell (Figure 4-24).

Organ

Electronic Organ

The electronic organ (such as the fun-luvin' Farfisa) is an electric instrument that can be recorded directly or plugged into an amp stack. As such, it can be treated much the same as an electric guitar.

If the electric organ is in a location, such as a church, where the speakers are built into the wall and the sound radiation is designed to

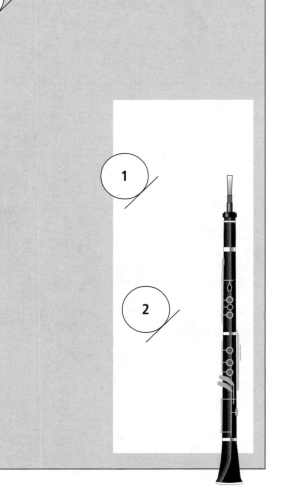

Figure 4-24
Oboe

1. If an oboe is encountered in a popular music setting, try miking it at a distance of 6"–2', placing the mic slightly above the player (Mic 1).

2. Pointing the mic slightly off to the side and at the middle of the body helps minimize breath noises (Mic 2).

3. For classical recording, the microphone should be placed slightly above the player, about 3–8' away, and aimed toward the middle of the body (Mic 3).

mimic a pipe organ, miking the room using traditional pipe organ recording techniques works well.

In R&B, soul, and popular music, the Hammond B3 and other electric organs are almost always plugged into a Leslie speaker. Its high and low rotating speaker mechanism add a Doppler swirl that causes a characteristic rise and drop in pitch (Figure 4-25).

Leslie Tips

- Dynamic microphones can capture the Leslie's gutsy gruff character, adding "beef" to a Hammond's sound. Condensers capture a clearer more present sound.
- The whirring sounds of the motors and baffles produce a lot of wind noise. Using a wind screen or pop filter helps reduce this. You might also want to experiment with mic placement.

Pipe Organ

Pipe organs are found in all sorts of environments, and one must generally record them where they're found. They range in size from lap sized medieval organs to huge ones, in great halls, that have hundreds of pipes. Due to the many different types and sizes of pipe organs, and the many different types of venues that they can be found in, a fair amount of experimentation may have to be done to capture the right sound.

Condenser mics are almost always pre-

Figure 4-25
Leslie Speaker Cabinet

The upper, high-frequency horn can be miked with either one or two mics (Mics 1 and 2) placed at a distance of 4–8" and panned to various degrees of left and right. Use another mic to capture the low-frequency speaker (Mic 3).

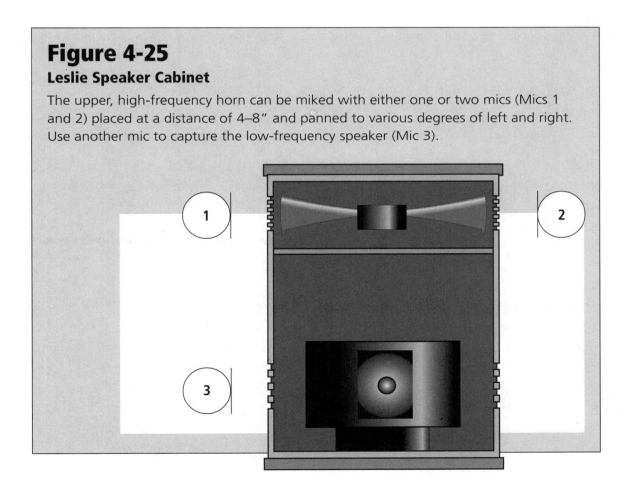

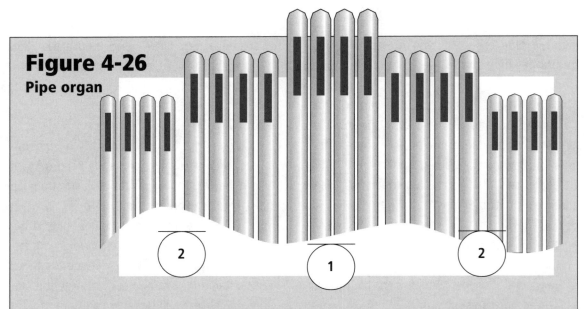

Figure 4-26
Pipe organ

1. The frequency range of the organ is perhaps the greatest found on any acoustic instrument. Typically, the organ is miked in stereo with a coincident stereo condenser pair (Mic Setup 1, CD Track 28) that are placed at a point providing the most balanced sound (often in the center of the instrument and at a height of 10' or more).

2. A spaced stereo pair of mics (Mic Setup 2, CD Track 28), placed midway between the instrument's center and outer edges will also produce good results. The distance from the pipes has to be determined by experiment, taking into account that most halls have reverberation problems to deal with. Often, a distance that's half the instrument's overall width will yield good results.

ferred due to their wide frequency response and ability to capture transients. Pipe organs can be very loud, especially up close, and it may be necessary to use the mic's pad to prevent overload (Figure 4-26).

Good results can often be easily obtained with a pair of boundary or PZM microphones in a stereo spaced pair configuration on the floor or side walls of the hall (CD Track 28).

Pipe Organ Tip

Miking a pipe organ is somewhat like miking an entire orchestra. If particular notes need to be picked up, or if the pipe sets are located such that there is no place where an even, balanced sound can be found for a single mic, accent mics

may need to be used in addition to the primary stereo pair. However, be very aware of potential phase pitfalls.

Pan Pipes

Pan pipes consist of a series of different length tubes that are played by blowing across the top of the pipes—the sound emanates primarily from this point. Their tone can be deep and penetrating, or it can be quite shrill. In either case, it's chock-full of high-frequency components and tends to have lots of breath sounds.

Use a mic with a good pop filter, positioned

at about the level of the player's forehead and aimed at the player's mouth from a distance of six inches for close pickup, or farther back if more room resonance is desired.

Percussion Instruments

Conga and Tumba

The conga and tumba are low-pitched, single-headed drums that physically differ only in their diameter (Figure 4-27).

If only one microphone is available, it can be aimed between the drums, placed 5–l0 inches away.

A deeper more bombastic sound can be obtained by miking the drums individually. Placing the mics close to the top head, about 1–3 inches above, and 2 inches in from the rim, produces a tight, dead sound with minimal shell resonance and enhanced head attack (Figure 4-27, Mics 1, CD Track 29). The mic distance above the head can be increased to about 10 inches to give a more "live" sound (Figure 4-27, Mics 2, CD Track 29).

Facing the capsules of two directional microphones at an opposing 45° angle improves both the separation and the stereo spread.

Conga and Tumba Tip

Often a dynamic mic with a midrange presence peak is used to mic these instruments.

Bongos

Two mics can be used to pickup bongos—about 1–2 inches above and one inch in from the rim—but usually a single microphone is placed between the two heads at a 5–10 inch, balanced distance.

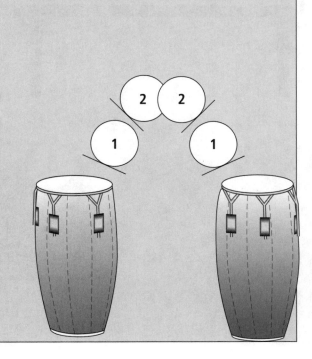

Figure 4-27
Conga drum

1. Placing the mics close to the top head, about 1–3" above, and 2" in from the rim, produces a tight, dead sound with minimal shell resonance and enhanced head attack (Mic Setup 1, CD Track 29).

2. The mic distance above the head can be increased to about 10" for a more "live" sound (Mic Setup 2, CD Track 29).

Percussion Toys

The percussionist's toy chest contains anything and everything from shakers, triangles, tambourines, bird whistles, maracas, all the way to little rubber frogs that squeak. These instruments generally have sharp, transient sounds that are best picked up with a high quality condenser or extended range dynamic mic.

Given adequate isolation from other instruments, a working distance of 1–4 feet is preferred in order to pick up some of the room's natural acoustics and to prevent microphone overload. A quieter instrument could be miked at a closer distance.

Tips on Toys

Some of these instruments can be quite loud, having overtones that continue above the hearing range. If necessary, you might want to pad the mic.

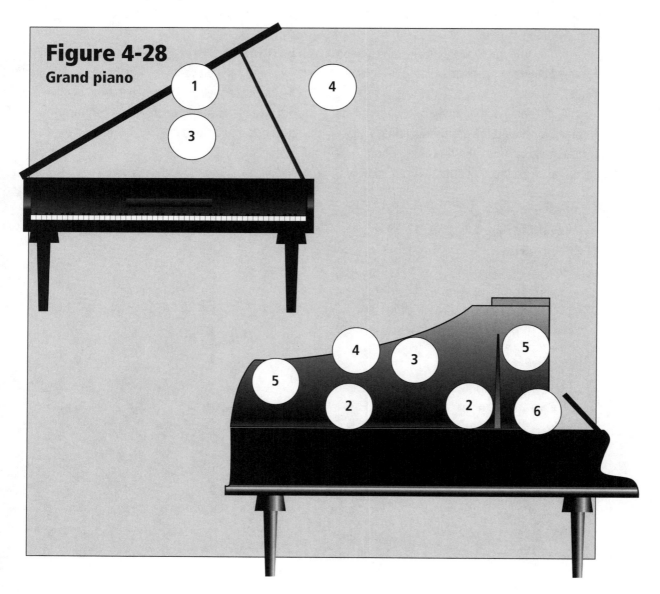

Figure 4-28
Grand piano

Grand Piano

The grand piano is the classic example of the principle of sound coming from many parts of an instrument. This is because the grand piano's sound generating surface is not only large, but it's also acoustically complex. As a result, there are about as many personal approaches to miking a piano as there are professional engineers.

The piano's sound, though often entrenched in tradition, has also evolved to include a contemporary style that's a compromise between a realistic sound, a percussive sound that can cut through a mix, and the necessity for acoustic separation from other instruments in the studio. As a result, a piano can be miked in any number of ways—depending on what is right for the given job (Figure 4-28).

Figure 4-28 shows some of the mic positions that are currently used to record a grand piano. Here are some guidelines to a proper balance, achieved through microphone choice and placement experimentation:

- One or two boundary mics can be attached to the piano's partially or completely opened lid. This method uses the lid as a collective reflector; it can sound good under restrictive conditions like on stage, in a live broadcast or wherever pickup visibility is a problem (Figure 4-28, Mic 1, CD Track 30).
- Two mics can be placed in a spaced stereo configuration (Figure 4-28, Mic Setup 2, CD Track 30) at a working distance of six inches to one foot, with one microphone centrally positioned over the low strings and the other placed over the high strings.
- A single coincident stereo pair can be positioned just inside the piano, between the soundboard and its fully or partially open lid (Figure 4-28, Mic Setup 3, CD Track 30).
- A single mic or coincident stereo pair can be placed outside the piano facing into the open lid. This method is most appropriate for solo or accent miking. It's also useful for classical recording, where the mic can be placed 7–25 feet or more away (Figure 4-28, Mic Setup 4, CD Track 30).
- A spaced stereo pair can be placed just outside the lid, facing into the instrument (Figure 4-28, Mic Setup 5, CD Track 30).
- A single microphone or coincident or spaced stereo pair can be positioned just over the piano hammers at a distance of 4–8 inches—a position that's often used to achieve a driving popular or rock sound (Figure 4-28, Mic Setup 6, CD Track 30).

Grand Piano Tips

- You generally want to raise the mics higher as you move farther from the piano.
- Condenser or extended range dynamic mics are usually chosen to mike an acoustic grand piano because they accurately represent the transient and complex nature of the instrument. When close-miking or isolation is required, a cardioid or tighter polar pattern can be used. Where leakage isn't a problem, an omnidirectional mic might be preferred to capture as much of the instrument as possible (this applies to single and spaced mic configurations). A boundary mic can be used wherever a sweet spot can be found (i.e., on the floor, wall, ceiling, etc.).
- Attention should be paid to room acoustics as well as to the piano itself (I'll bet ya can't tuna fish?). In classical recording, artificial reverberation might not be needed since the relatively distant miking techniques, often

preferred in this genre, typically capture plenty of room reverberation: this isn't a hard and fast rule, particularly if the room's reverb doesn't sound very good. Watch for reflections from the ceiling and walls. If more than one mic is used, check for phase cancellation or comb filter problems by bringing up the second mic and listening for frequency dropouts in mono.

Separation

Achieving separation is often a problem when the grand piano is placed next to raucous musical neighbors. Any of these methods can improve your separation problems:

- Place the piano inside an isolation booth.
- Place a movable sound isolating partition (a.k.a.: flat, gobo, or baffle) between the piano and its loudest neighbor.
- Place the mics inside the piano and either lower the lid onto its short stick or close it entirely. A heavy moving blanket or a regular blanket can be placed over the lid to further reduce leakage: this technique works best when close-miking.
- Overdub the instrument at a later time. In this instance, the lid can be propped up by the long stick with the mics placed at a more natural sounding distance.

Upright Piano

You would expect the techniques for this seemingly harmless type of piano to be similar to its larger brother. This is generally true; but, since this piano was designed for home enjoyment and not performance, the techniques employed are slightly different, and it's often more difficult to achieve a respectable tone quality (Figure 4-29).

In close-miking the upright piano, two factors need to be kept in mind:

1. Because of the piano's design, access to its strings may be restricted, limiting microphone placement.
2. Distant- and sometimes even close-miking tends to produce a muddy sound when the upright is recorded in a small room.

Try these approaches to miking the upright piano:

- **Miking over the top**: Place two mics in a 3:1 fashion just over the piano's open top— one over the bass strings and the other over the treble strings (Figure 4-29, Mic Setup 1, CD Track 31). If isolation isn't a factor, remove or open the front face (which covers the strings) in order to reduce reflections and thus the instrument's boxy quality.
- **Miking the soundboard**: To reduce excessive hammer attack, remove the front face and place a microphone pair about eight inches from the soundboard, covering the bass and treble strings (Figure 4-29, Mic Setup 2, CD Track 31). Another technique involves removing the front face and pointing a single or coincident stereo mic over the player's head, facing the middle of the dampers (Figure 4-29, Mic 3, CD Track 31). Alternatively, use two mics about 2–3 feet away from the strings: one pointing toward the treble and the other toward the bass strings.
- **Miking the kickboard area**: For a more natural sound, remove the kickboard (at the lower front part of the piano) so the strings are exposed. Place a stereo spaced pair over the strings about eight inches over the bass and treble strings (Figure 4-29, Mic Setup 4, CD Track 31). If only one mic can be spared, place it over the treble end.
- **Boundary miking**: Boundary microphones

Figure 4-29
Upright piano

"You would expect the techniques for this seemingly harmless type of piano to be similar to its larger brother. This is generally true; but, since this piano was designed for home enjoyment and not performance, the techniques employed are slightly different, and it's often more difficult to achieve a respectable tone quality."

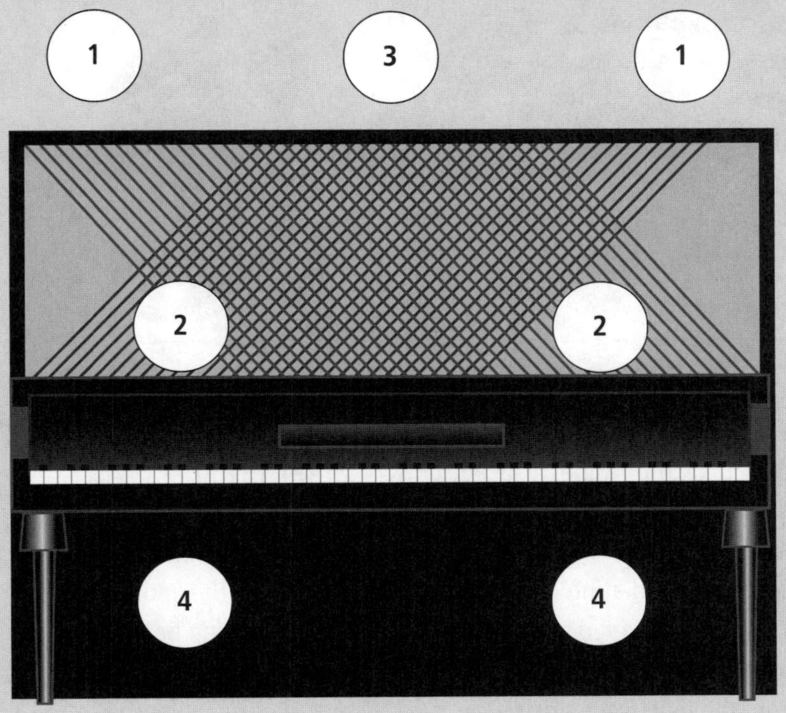

often work well on upright pianos, although placement varies with environment and instrument. To begin, the mic(s) can be affixed to the nearest large boundary or to the top lid, which can be closed for isolation. Moving the piano about 1 1/2 feet out from the wall and placing a pair of boundary microphones on the wall at the piano's half-height point, about four feet apart and straddling the middle of the soundboard, can provide some surprising results (CD Track 31).

Saxophone

Saxophones vary greatly in size and shape. The most popular models for rock and jazz are the "S" curved B-flat tenor sax, whose fundamentals span from B2 to F5 (177–725 Hz), and the E-flat alto, with a span from C3 to G5 (140–784 Hz). Also in this family are the straight tube soprano and the "S" shaped baritone and bass saxophone. Playing technique affects the

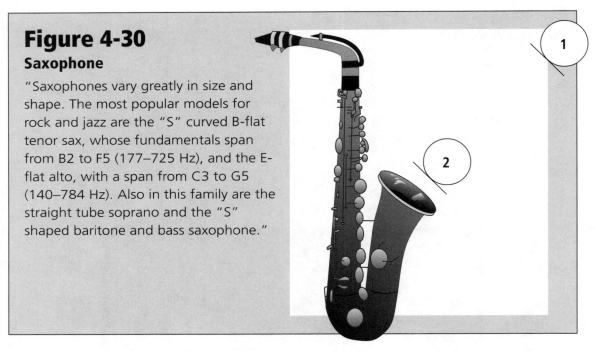

Figure 4-30
Saxophone

"Saxophones vary greatly in size and shape. The most popular models for rock and jazz are the "S" curved B-flat tenor sax, whose fundamentals span from B2 to F5 (177–725 Hz), and the E-flat alto, with a span from C3 to G5 (140–784 Hz). Also in this family are the straight tube soprano and the "S" shaped baritone and bass saxophone."

harmonic content of the instrument, which generally runs up to 8 kHz and is extended by breath noises that take the range to a peak between 12 and 13 kHz (Figure 4-30).

Unlike the rest of the woodwinds, the saxophone is a closed system, radiating much of its sound from the bell. For the curved saxophones, the mic can be pointed at the instrument about 3–6 inches up from the bell, from a distance of about a foot (Figure 4-30, Mic 1, CD Track 32).

The soprano sax, which is straight, is miked about a foot from the instrument with the mic pointing about 3–8 inches up from the bell.

Keypad noises are considered a part of the instruments sound, but aiming the microphone at the outer rim of the bell may eliminate even those (Figure 4-30, Mic 2, CD Track 32).

Sax Tip
In the above examples, a good quality condenser mic should be used.

Steel Drum

The steel drum is often a collection of tuned oil drums (or the more expensive manufactured types) that can be miked much like a set of timpani or drum overheads. Since steel drums don't take well to being close-miked, it's preferable to mic individual drums at a distance of 1–3 feet above the head, depending upon leakage factors with nearby steel drums and/or other instruments (Figure 4-31, Mic 1).

Since a good deal of the steel drum sound radiates downward from the head, you could also place a microphone facing up, about one foot below the instrument (Figure 4-31, Mic 2). This placement could reduce leakage problems while providing a closer and more immediate sound.

Since these instruments are usually played in groups of two or four, a pair can often share

Figure 4-31
Steel drum

"Since these instruments are usually played in groups of two or four, a pair can often share a microphone in order to reduce phase errors. You could also use a spaced or coincident stereo pair at a distance of 3–4 feet above the grouped drums. Pulling back to a further distance introduces more of the room's sound into the mix."

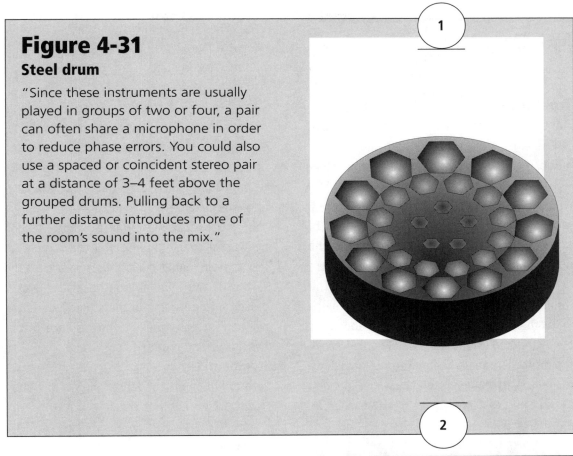

a microphone in order to reduce phase errors. You could also use a spaced or coincident stereo pair at a distance of 3–4 feet above the grouped drums. Pulling back to a further distance introduces more of the room's sound into the mix.

Steel Guitar and Lap Steel

The steel guitar and lap steel are electric instruments that have about the same tonal range as the electric guitar. They're generally miked the same as electric guitar—often with a rugged sounding dynamic, such as a Shure SM57.

Timpani

Capable of low sustained rumblings as well as loud transient bangs, timpani are among the most commonly used drums in classical music.

As the stretched membrane works together with a kettle shell to produce the overall sound, these instruments sound best when miked at a distance of 1 1/2 feet or more over the top (CD Track 33). Timpani are often played in groups of two or four. A pair may share a microphone in order to reduce phase errors.

Basic Brass

Trombone

The trombone comes in an assortment of sizes and is most often found in jazz and classical music. The tenor is most common; its fundamental range falls between E2 and C5 (82 and 520 Hz) with an output that's rich with overtones. Medium loud playing gives an upper limit of 5 kHz while harder blowing could press the upper limit to 10 kHz. Typical formants are at 480–600 Hz and around 1.2 kHz. The trombone's polar pattern is nearly as symmetrical as the trumpet's. Below 400 Hz, frequencies are distributed evenly while at 2 kHz and above the dispersion angle is down to 45° on axis to the bell. With extremely loud passages, the dispersion angle at and above 7 kHz can be as narrow as 20°.

A jazz trombone is often miked at a distance of two inches to two feet, slightly to the side of the bell: from the player's standpoint,

they should play slightly to the side of the mic. As with trumpet, the danger of overload is present, so you might want to consider using a pad (CD Track 34).

In miking a trombone section, a single microphone can be placed between two players, with each pair in the section being mixed down to a stereo sub-mix or (if available) recorded onto their own tracks for mixdown at a later time.

In classical music, the trombone section needs the spacious ensemble blending that results from longer miking distances. Treat the section as an overall part of the ensemble or, if broken into a section in the studio, you might want to increase your miking distance to between two and four feet.

Trombone Tip

Large diaphragm condenser mics and ribbon mics work well on trombone.

Trumpet

The trumpet contains overtones that stretch up to 15 kHz. Its fundamental frequencies lie be-

Figure 4-32
Trumpet

"Because of the high sound pressure levels that can be encountered during a trumpet passage (up to 155 dB SPL), it's best to place a mic slightly off-center to the bell, at a distance of 1' or more. When closer placement is needed, a 10–20 dB pad can be inserted to prevent mic overload. Under such close working conditions, a windscreen helps protect the diaphragm from excessive windblasts"

tween E3 and D6 (165 Hz to 1.175 kHz). Below 500 Hz, the sound projects uniformly in all directions; at 1.5 kHz and up, the projected sound becomes highly directional; above 5 kHz, the dispersion angle is a tight 30° on axis to the bell. The trumpet's formants—the relative harmonic levels that produce its specific character—fall at points around 1–1.5 kHz and at 2–3 kHz. Using a mute radically changes its tone. A cup-shaped mute, that fits over the bell, dampens frequencies above 2.5 kHz, while a conical mute, which fits inside the bell, cuts back on the region below 1.5 kHz and emphasizes the spectrum above 4 kHz (Figure 4-32).

Because of the high sound pressure levels that can be encountered during a trumpet passage (up to 155 dB SPL), it's best to place a mic slightly off-center to the bell, at a distance of one foot or more. When closer placement is needed, a 10–20 dB pad can be inserted to prevent mic overload. Under such close working conditions, a windscreen helps protect the diaphragm from excessive windblasts: this especially holds true for older ribbon designs.

Due to its strong harmonic structure, the sound of a trumpet can be shaped by the choice of microphone.

A condenser mic accurately captures the instrument's transient response (Mic 1, CD Track 35).

A dynamic mic smooths out the transients by rounding them off (Mic 2, CD Track 35). In addition, its rugged design can be useful in situations where physical damage is a possibility.

A ribbon mic—particularly of the older variety—can be close-miked to provide a mellow high-end response and proximity effect, both of which can give the instrument a fuller tone (Mic 3, CD Track 35).

Trumpet Tip

Since the trumpet contains high-level transient peaks, it's a good idea to keep the recorded signal at levels between -6 and 0 VU (at least -12 on most digital meters) in order to reduce the possibility of tape saturation or digital overload.

Tuba

The bass and double bass tubas are the lowest pitched of the brass instruments. The range of the bass tuba is actually a fifth higher than the double bass; however, it's still possible to obtain a low fundamental of B (29 Hz!). The overtone structure is limited, with the top response ranging from 1.5–2 kHz. The lower frequencies of the tuba (around 75 Hz) are spread evenly; as the frequencies rise, the off-axis distribution angle reduces drastically.

Normally, this class of instruments isn't miked at close distances; a working range of two feet or more, slightly off axis to the bell, yields the best results. A large-diaphragm condenser mic will pick up the attack, but a vintage ribbon mic can provide a smoother bottom end pickup. Some engineers use both the condenser and ribbon, side by side, blending them to shape the final sound.

Ukulele

The ukulele is like a very small guitar with four nylon strings. It's generally played in a strumming fashion with the fingers and can, from a recording standpoint, be treated like an acoustic guitar.

Mike it over the fingerboard, where it joins the body, with a small-diaphragm condenser mic positioned 6–12 inches away.

Violin and Viola

A high quality condenser mic that displays as flat a frequency response as possible should be used to record violin. The violin's frequency range runs from 200 Hz to 10 kHz and its fundamental pitch range is from G3 to E6 (200 Hz to 1.3 kHz). It's particularly important that the mic be flat within the formant frequencies of 300 Hz, 1 kHz and 1.2 kHz. The fundamental range of the viola is a fifth lower and contains fewer harmonic overtones than the violin (Figure 4-33).

Up to 500 Hz, the sound radiation of the violin is uniform. Above this point, the sound projection is concentrated in a direction perpendicular to the top soundboard. As the overall frequency dispersion is approximately 15° to the instrument's front face, the microphone is generally placed directly in line with this angle and pointed at the strings and the f holes at a distance of 1–3 feet (Figure 4-33, Mic 1, CD Track 36).

As miking distance decreases, a scratchy nasal quality is often picked up. For a solo instrument, the microphone should be placed between three and eight feet away, positioned slightly above and in front of the player (Figure 4-33, Mic 2, CD Track 36).

Under solo studio conditions, a more immediate sound can be gotten by placing the mic within four inches to one foot of the body, at a position just below the bridge, pointing toward the strings (Figure 4-33, Mic 3, CD Track 36).

Fiddle and Jazz/Rock Violin

A fiddle is no different from a violin, except that fiddle players generally use steel strings and go

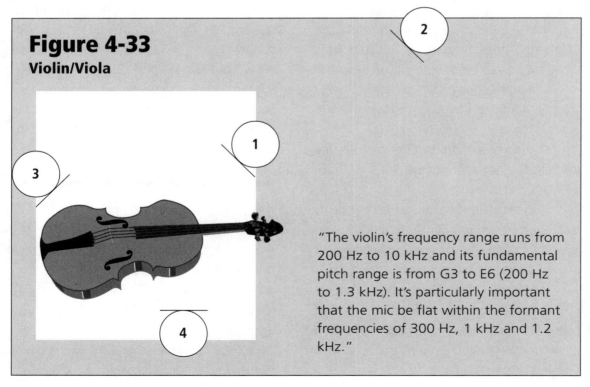

Figure 4-33
Violin/Viola

"The violin's frequency range runs from 200 Hz to 10 kHz and its fundamental pitch range is from G3 to E6 (200 Hz to 1.3 kHz). It's particularly important that the mic be flat within the formant frequencies of 300 Hz, 1 kHz and 1.2 kHz."

for a different sound than classical violinists. Some fiddle players are quite smooth, producing a good tone—generally without the vibrato that's associated with the violin.

For a fiddle or jazz/rock violin, the mic can be placed as close as six inches away: though a more typical distance for a fiddle is about 18 inches. While the mic most often is aimed at approximately the end of the fingerboard, a good sound can be obtained by aiming it at the player's chin (Figure 4-33, Mic 1, CD Track 37).

The instrument's bottom end can be accentuated by adding a mic at the back of the fiddle—usually with a small-diaphragm condenser microphone—and blending it with the front mic as needed (Figure 4-33, Mics 2 and 4, CD Track 37). Remember to watch for phase problems.

Many fiddlers use pickups on their instruments. These never sound as good as a miked fiddle, but may deliver a sound that the fiddler desires. In this case, treat the fiddle as an electric instrument and use a DI—or mic the instrument and mix it in with the DI. It's generally a good idea to avoid small condenser mics that are clipped onto the instrument, since these

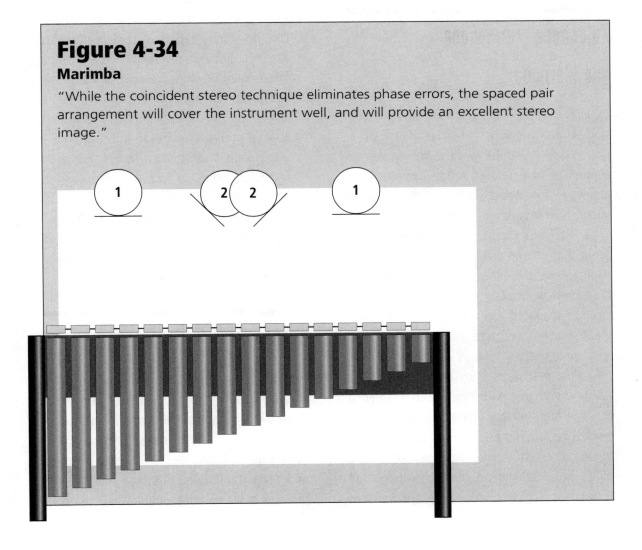

Figure 4-34
Marimba

"While the coincident stereo technique eliminates phase errors, the spaced pair arrangement will cover the instrument well, and will provide an excellent stereo image."

pick up the instrument's scraping sounds and the musician's breathing.

Fiddle Tips

- Sometimes a fiddler also sings into the fiddle mic. In this case, it's usually necessary to mic the fiddle close enough to pick up the vocal, with appropriate balance between the fiddle and vocal.

- Since some fiddlers play with a quite harsh, scratchy tone, a more pleasing recorded sound can be obtained with a vintage ribbon microphone, like an RCA DX-44, that rolls off the high frequencies.

Xylophone, Vibraphone and Marimba

The common technique used for tuned percussion instruments such as the xylophone, vibraphone and marimba is to place two good condenser or extended range dynamic mics about one foot above the playing bars, spaced about three feet apart (Figure 4-34, Mic Setup 1, CD Track 38). Or, use a coincident stereo mic setup that has an offset angle of about 135° (Figure 4-34, Mic Setup 2, CD Track 38). While the coincident stereo technique eliminates phase errors, the spaced pair arrangement will cover the instrument well, and will provide an excellent stereo image.

Folk marimbas, such as those found in Africa, Southeast Asia, and Central America produce high volume levels and have lots of resonance. Often these instruments are played in ensembles, which you might want to pick up as a whole, rather than close-miking any one instrument. Typically, folk marimba ensembles

are miked using a stereo miking technique to get a good ensemble balance (See Chapter 6).

If you want to record an ensemble using multitrack techniques, mic each instrument with a pair of cardioid mics, as closely as possible, while getting a balanced sound for the entire instrument. You'll probably want to space the instruments apart and angle the mics, so as to minimize leakage between instruments. Don't forget to watch for phase problems, occasionally monitoring your mix in mono.

Marimba Tips

- Miking from underneath gives a less-defined sound and picks up more room leakage.

- Room acoustics can be a major factor in recording ethnic marimbas. Some performers like recording in a reverberant room, with a fair amount of room pickup. Some of these groups can be miked effectively with just a single pair of boundary mics on the floor in spaced stereo configuration, since these instruments often cause a smaller live room to sound boomy. In such a case, acoustical absorption may be needed.

- As with all ethnic and folk performers, find out from the performer what is desired and use your general knowledge of single mic and stereo techniques to get it.

Zither

The European zither has a fingerboard for playing chords and a course of strings for playing accompaniment. It's generally played on a table, or on the lap, and is often quiet and harmonically complex. The general design and temperament of this instrument often requires a bit of forethought with regard to mic technique.

A pickup can be placed at a distance between six inches and three feet, depending on instrument and conditions. Often a coincident stereo mic best represents the instrument's subtle colors.

Zither Tips

• Because its signal output is very low, you might be tempted to close-mike the zither; however, an overall blend is essential to its sound—sometimes requiring that a semi-distant technique be used. This often leads to problems with leakage from other instruments onto the softer zither tracks. This problem can be solved in the studio by isolating the instrument, or by overdubbing it at a later time, when it can be played on its own.

• When miking the zither, a condenser mic is often the best choice because of the instrument's harmonic complexity.

Chapter 5 Miking Vocals and Speech

There are many types of vocalists and many ways of recording them. The way that works best for a rock lead singer might not work at all well for a "crooner", a folk or ethnic performer, or a classical singer. As with every recording situation, your first job should be to determine the sound that the vocalist and/or producer wants for the particular production. It's also a wise idea to listen to the voice for awhile and become familiar with the general volume level, projection, dynamic range, frequency range, and any special problems—such as sibilance or popping—that the vocalist might have.

Some singers, such as rock vocalists, classical singers, and lead gospel performers can really belt it out, while other singers can be quite soft. Sometimes, our job might be to mic the vocalist so they sound natural and lifelike; at other times, you might want to augment or alter their sound via special mic and electronic techniques.

If it's at all possible, listen to a recording that's furnished by the vocalist to illustrate the sound that they'd like to get. This can help give you a reference point from which to start. By using the available tools, in even a minimally equipped studio, and by being willing to experiment, you can often duplicate a particular sound—sometimes even from a relatively inexperienced singer. Nothing, however, can correct for a singer who sings badly out of tune

or gives a bad performance. Some tweaking of the sound is possible, but a bad performance can't be fixed in the mix.

Singing is one of the most ego sensitive ways of making music. Singers are putting themselves on the line to a greater extent, psychologically, than most instrumentalists. To get a good vocal performance, the psychological needs of the vocalist must first be met. One rule to follow, and to use as a maxim in vocal recording, is to give the vocalist positive reinforcement at all times and not be critical of the performance in a way that the vocalist could interpret simply as destructive criticism. A statement such as "Now you're getting it; let's do another take and make it even better" will be taken in a better light than "That sucks; you've got to do it again." It also helps to create a comfortable environment in the studio. This may mean getting rid of clutter and cleaning the place so it's dust and allergen free, creating a pleasant looking space, or dimming the lights and using candles for ambience—anything and everything that makes the singer feel comfortable and inspired. Finding out in advance the kind of environment that the vocalist likes, and striving to create it, can go a long way toward capturing a great performance.

Another biggie that's often overlooked is time! Vocalists sometimes need lots of it, and since the lead vocal is often the last track to be laid down before mixing, it's all to easy to overlook their need, running out of time or money before the vocalist walks in! Our advice is **don't**! You, and especially the producer, should take the time to acquaint yourselves with the vocalist. Is this One Take Sally, or will it require 10 or more takes, plus several punch-ins? Don't forget that even One Take Sally can have a bad day. Give yourselves enough time to smooth out the frays, or even call the session off till a better day. Remember, once its on tape, you may be stuck with it: it's always better to do it right.

OK, let's get back to the session at hand. If the vocalist is overdubbing, they'll most likely be wearing headphones to hear a guide mix of the song. It's important that you give the vocalist a headphone mix that they'll feel comfortable singing along with. The final result and overall feel that the vocalist will project in the song is often worth the time taken.

In most cases, the vocalist will be listening to both themselves—along with a bit of added reverb—and the backing instruments in the headphones. If the singer's level is high in the headphones, they might sing softer to bring their level in the headphones down. If you want them to sing loud, turn them down in the headphone mix. If you want them to sing real loud—such as for a rock screamer—turn up the instrument mix in the headphones and turn down the vocalist, so they'll have to scream to hear themselves. The vocalist also picks up pitch cues from this mix. For example, if it's too bassy, the singer will often tend to sing flat.

If the headphones don't seal around the vocalist's ears, and are too loud, the vocal mic might pick up the mix. Listen carefully for this, as bleed from the headphones can cause problems with the vocal recording, especially during quiet vocal passages or when the vocalist stops singing for an instrumental lick or break.

Voice Characteristics

From shout to whisper, the human voice displays dynamics and timbre that few other instruments can approach. The male bass voice can extend from E2 to D4 (82 to 293 Hz) with harmonics extending to 7 kHz. Sibilant "s" and "th" sounds often extend to 12 kHz. The upper soprano voice can range up to 1.05 kHz with harmonics that climb to 9 kHz. In addition, the vowel sounds (a, e, i, o and u) are formed when the mouth takes a particular shape, creating formants—strongly emphasized resonance bands which occur even if the pitch varies.

You should be aware of four traps that can be encountered when recording the human voice:
1. Having a vocalist with a dynamic range that's too much for the recording chain.
2. Sibilants (f, s, sh and ch), can be overly accentuated.
3. Plosive "p" sounds can create unwanted popping at the mic diaphragm.
4. Excessive bass boosts can occur due to proximity effect.

Dynamic Range

One of the significant problems in vocal miking and recording is a signal that has too wide a dynamic range for the recorded medium. For example, let's assume that an average vocal level is recorded on tape at approximately 0 VU (+4 dBm), while on occasion the vocalist will belt out a level that's 12 dB higher. This would cause the system to attempt the recording of a +16 dBm signal on tape. Since the maximum level that can be recorded varies from about +8 dBm for a pro analog deck, to a lot less for a digital machine, such a signal would result in severe distortion. For this reason, it's necessary to reduce the level of these loud passages to a more manageable level through the use of a dynamic range changer, such as the compressor.

Sibilance

The sibilant sounds can easily become distorted when recorded at too high a level or at too slow a tape speed. Certain mics that contain upper-frequency peaks can easily exaggerate these sibilant sounds. A frequency-selective limiter, known as a de-esser, which can sense and reduce excessive sibilance at its output, can correct this problem. The problem can also be tackled (with a lesser degree of dynamic intelligence) by cutting frequencies in the 7–9 kHz region with an equalizer.

Popping

When placed at close working distances, most directional microphones display an increased sensitivity to low-frequency signals. The most obtrusive of these signals are the plosive sounds (p, t, k, b, d and g) that can create a loud pop that's caused by the sudden rush of air at the front of the mic's diaphragm. This problem can be tackled in three ways:

1. Place a foam windscreen or a nylon mesh pop filter over the front face of the mic grille. This serves as a barrier to the high-pressure popping energy while allowing the sound to pass.
2. Substitute a directional mic for an omnidirectional one. Omnis are less effected by sudden bursts in pressure and might be the best pattern choice if excessive leakage isn't a problem.
3. Place the mic well above or to the side of the mouth.

Proximity Effect

It's a well-known fact that, at close distances, most directional mics boost the bass frequencies. This effect can be either negative or positive, depending upon the results you want. For example, over the decades, bass boost due to proximity effect has been a distinctive part of a vocalist's and radio announcer's sound. It adds a rich, deep sexiness that tends to fill the tone out, while making the sound more immediate.

All directional mics have proximity effect to some degree—unless they're specially engineered to reduce it. If this boost isn't desired, try moving the vocalist at least 5–8 inches away from a directional mic, or roll off the bass frequencies at the mic, or reduce low frequencies at the input strip by inserting a bass roll-off, or simply use an equalizer. It might surprise you to know that using an omni mic instead of a directional one will also eliminate this bass boost.

Mic Selection

The best microphone for recording vocals depends on the sound you want, the type of vocal that you're recording, and the recording environment. Each of the mic types has its own characteristics that make it desirable or undesirable for achieving a particular vocal sound. There's often no one microphone that's best for every vocal recording situation. Certain mic types have become fairly standard in the industry for special vocal applications. Understanding the differences between mic types and experimenting with them can give you valuable insights into capturing just the right vocal sound. You might find, through your own experimentation, that the mic that would seem to be the obvious choice doesn't do as good a job as you might expect, and vice-versa.

Dynamic Mics

A dynamic mic often provides a warm rugged sound which can be categorized as present or dirty. The presence is often a product of a peak in the upper-mid frequencies that helps the sound cut through a mix. This mid boost can be filled out with the help of a close proximity bass boost. Many dynamic vocal mics are designed to be used quite close, often with the vocalist's mouth touching the windscreen. Some vocalists are used to singing into these mics, keeping their vocal output at a fairly low level and using the mic's sound and proximity effect to give them a characteristic sound.

Ribbon Mics

Ribbon microphones are the classic "crooner" and "announcer" mic. They generally have a good transient response and tons of proximity effect, which combine to give them a smooth mellow sound. The best results can be obtained at a working distance of 4–6 inches. Ribbon mics that are used at greater distances will produce their characteristically smooth sound without much bass boost.

Many of the great vocal soloist recordings of the swing and early jazz and blues eras were made with ribbon mics that were placed about two feet in front of the singer, just a little higher than stomach level, tilted up to point at the vocalist's mouth. Other great classic swing, jazz,

and blues vocals were recorded with a ribbon mic on a boom above the vocalist's head, tilted down. Ribbon mics are particularly sensitive to air blowing on the ribbon, and can be destroyed by a good blast of air. Often they're used slightly above, below, or to the side of the vocalist to prevent such blasts.

Condenser Mics

Condenser mics are most often used in studio vocal work. Some of the classic tube condenser mics are sought after for the unique sound they impart to vocals. Although most of them are priced above what many mere music mortals can afford, several manufacturers offer new tube condenser mics that are designed to imitate characteristics of the classic mics, or they offer different characteristics the manufacturers believe can help create a new standard. These classic and neoclassic vocal mics are of the large-diaphragm type. These large-diaphragm, condenser mics produce an open and clear vocal sound that's extremely accurate. All of this isn't to say that small-diaphragm condenser mics don't work well on vocals: they do, especially when you want a clear, present sound—often desired when recording female vocalists.

Condensers are particularly prone to popping from vocal air blasts and—unless the vocalist is trained to avoid singing directly into the mic—need to be used with a wind screen or pop filter.

A number of classic crooners understand that, on soft passages, you can sing very close to the mic—to get a warm bass quality without using a windscreen—by singing the passages right under the mic with the mic diaphragm at about nose level, directing their wind downward. You'll often see them step back and turn their head just slightly away from the mic when they're about to belt out a passage. All this is possible because condensers generally have a great pickup range and can be used effectively at different distances by a singer who knows how to work the distances to the best effect.

During a loud passage, it's possible for a vocalist to overload the mic's internal preamp (especially on a large-diaphragm, condenser mic), making it necessary to switch its attenuation pad into the circuit. Overload can be a problem when a mic is used to pick up both an acoustic instrument and the voice. The mic can overload if the vocal output is greater than the instrument's when the mic setup is positioned between the two to get a good balance. Sometimes this overload is only slight and difficult to detect, so you might want to listen to the vocal

with the pad out, and then with the pad in, and see if it cleans up the sound.

Frequency Response Characteristics and Equalization

As we stated earlier, many vocal mics are designed to have a slight boost in the 2–3 kHz ranges. This intentional modification gives the mic an added presence on stage and helps the vocalist stand out from the instrumental backup. This may or may not be desired in recording; you might want to record the vocals with a mic that has a reasonably flat frequency response, later adding any presence boosts, during mixdown, with an equalizer.

Figure 5-1
Placement of the Cardioid Mic at Close Working Distances

"Sometimes the singer's lips need to be right on the wind screen: other times they need to be 18" or more from the mic. If the vocalist naturally works very close to the mic, there may be little choice of what mic to use and where to place it. Working with a vocalist that's willing to experiment gives you more options."

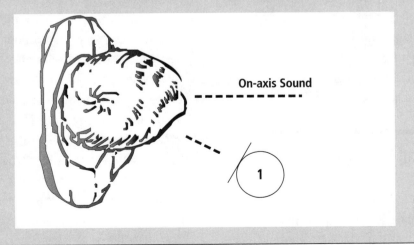

Figure 5-2
Two-microphone Soloist Technique

"Often the accent mic is placed at a slightly higher level, in line with the closer mic. As with all multiple mic techniques, you should be aware of the possible phasing problems that could crop up."

If it's obvious that the vocal quality is improved by adjusting the frequency response, you might consider using mic placement to accomplish this, rather than an equalizer. For example, if a deeper bass range is what you want, try a directional mic that has lots of proximity effect. A thin sounding voice can often be improved by placing the mic off axis to the voice to roll off the high end. Recording the vocal with flat frequency response gives you the opportunity to equalize the vocal track for the best effect during mixdown.

Miking Lead Vocals

How you might want to record a lead vocal will, again, depend on the sound that you want and the type of music that's being recorded. Some-

times the singer's lips need to be right on the wind screen: other times they need to be 18 inches or more from the mic. If the vocalist naturally works very close to the mic, there may be little choice of what mic to use and where to place it. Working with a vocalist that's willing to experiment gives you more options.

From a practical point of view, it's common to mount a mic on a boom arm that can safely be suspended in front of the vocalist so the diaphragm is about at nose level, pointing at the vocalist's mouth—you might want to use a pop filter. The distance from the mic to the vocalist depends, to a great extent, on the vocalist's projection and the type of music that's being used to record. Typical distances are 8–12 inches. A soft vocalist or a crooner can move in closer and sing just under the mic. For loud passages, the vocalist can back away, tilt the head back slightly, and sing directly at the mic. A loud lead singer might even record at further distances (Figure 5-1).

It's interesting to note that a vocalist needs a minimum of about 26 dB isolation from other instruments in order to keep leakage or bleeding under control. Depending upon the volume levels of both the vocalist and the instrument(s), the vocalist in a reasonable studio must be at least 8–16 feet away from another sound source—if no baffling is used.

Two-Microphone Soloist Technique

Sometimes a solo or accent microphone that's placed 2–8 feet away can be used in conjunction with the primary mic to fill out a vocalist's sound. In the case when a trained singer has lots of projection, a close mic can be used to capture overall clarity and presence; however, a distant mic will sometimes add depth and subtlety to the pickup. Often the accent mic is placed at a slightly higher level, in line with the closer mic. As with all multiple mic techniques, you should be aware of the possible phasing problems that could crop up (Figure 5-2).

Backup Vocals

Backup vocals can be recorded all at once or overdubbed one voice at a time. The latter might be necessary if the vocalists have difficulty finding and holding their respective parts, and need to repeat their performance over and over, punching in to get it right. In this case, each track can be dealt with as though you're recording a soloist. By far, the usual (and best) practice, is to use vocalists that are well prepared, well rehearsed, and who can all sing together live to one or more tracks or pair of tracks.

If you have lots of available tracks, or if bouncing tracks down to a stereo sub-mix is no problem, you could simply give each vocalist his or her own mic—making sure to follow the basic 3:1 distance rule to avoid leakage and phasing problems. As an alternative, all singers can be gathered around a single omnidirectional mic or a coincident stereo pair. Using this approach, the relative positions of each singer can be physically adjusted until the best vocal blend is achieved (Figure 5-3).

On the positive side, the vocalists can stand around an omni mic, using visual cues (as well as those from the headphone mix) to help shape their performance. On the downside, the one mic method takes more work on the part of the vocalists, and the blend can't be fixed in the mix. Even so, it's often well worth the effort to get the team working as a single instrument. On a final note, room acoustics need to be taken into account to see that reflections don't interfere with the clarity of the recording.

Choral Miking

Choruses or choirs can be miked with a spaced microphone pair that's placed in front of the chorus to the left and right of the centerline. Finding the proper place for these mics might take some experimentation. Listen to the group perform, then move forward and back in line with the center of the group until you find a pickup distance that seems right to you. Mark this spot, and envision an imaginary line, running parallel to the chorus at this distance. Then, start by placing mics to the left and right along this line, spacing each mic between the center-

Figure 5-3
Backup Vocal Recording With One Omnidirectional Mic

"On the positive side, the vocalists can stand around an omni mic, using visual cues (as well as those from the headphone mix) to help shape their performance.

...the one mic method takes more work on the part of the vocalists, and the blend can't be fixed in the mix. Even so, it's often well worth the effort to get the team working as a single instrument."

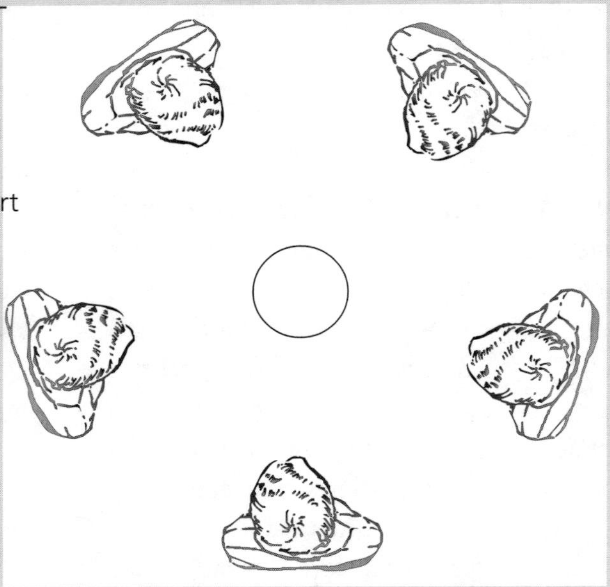

line and the respective end of the chorus (Figure 5-4, Mic Setup 1). Next, move the mics backward and forward, and in and out until you get the sound you like: moving the mics closer to the centerline will tighten up the stereo image and avoid a hole in the middle. Point the mics up and down, and slightly to one side or the other, to adjust the balance between the singers. Don't forget to keep the 3:1 rule in mind, listening for phase cancellation problems and excessive room reverb (See Chapter 6, *Stereo Miking*).

Another approach for stereo miking a chorus is to use an X-Y coincident pair (Figure 5-4, Mic Setup 2). Locate the cardioid pair in front of the chorus, as high as is practical, within the confines of the room, and direct the center axis of the two mics towards the center of the chorus. Once done, you can move them forward or back, and even from side to side, until you get the balance you want.

A matched pair of high quality directional mics with good off-axis response should be used; these should be placed far enough back to eliminate off-axis coloration. If they're placed too close for the size of the group, some of the pickup will either be completely off axis or it'll be off axis enough for the sound to be colored.

A single mic can also be used for chorus recording. This can likewise be placed along the centerline of the chorus, as high as possible and pointed down at just below the top row. It can be moved forward and back, and angled to achieve the blend that you want. The major problem with a single mic is that you can easily pick up too much reverberation from a live room, since the mic may have to be positioned farther back than a mic pair to pick up the entire chorus equally.

Speech Miking

The first and foremost goal in speech recording is to make the speech intelligible so the listener doesn't have to strain to understand the words. A second and more subliminal goal might be to enhance the voice, to project authority or intimacy to get across the spoken message.

Most speech sounds fall in the frequency range between 100 and 500 Hz. Overtones from the male voice range up to about 8 kHz, and for the female voice to about 10 kHz, with intelligibility coming from the higher frequencies.

All three mic types are commonly used for speech recording. The type of mic and how you want to use it depends, to a great extent, on the recording situation and the speaker. Again, the goal is to achieve the sound desired while preserving the intelligibility.

In practice, close-miking speech might pick up too much breathing and teeth noise, but it's often necessary in a noisy environment. Miking from too great a distance can make a voice

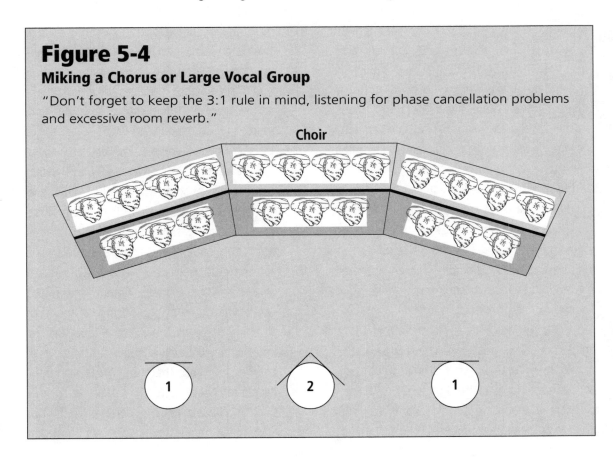

Figure 5-4
Miking a Chorus or Large Vocal Group

"Don't forget to keep the 3:1 rule in mind, listening for phase cancellation problems and excessive room reverb."

Choir

1   2   1

sound hollow, lacking presence. Typical mic distances range from very close (with the mouth being right on a foam windscreen) to somewhat distant (with the mouth being up to two feet away). Recording speech for video or stage might require that highly directional mics be used at various distances, or that wireless lapel mics be used.

The speaker should generally be placed on axis to the mic. However, good results can also be achieved by having the talent either speak across the mic from the side, or remain on axis to the mic, speaking to the side of it. If there are no extraneous noises to eliminate, and proximity effect bass boost isn't a problem, you might want to use an omni mic. In a noisy environment, a directional mic should be used. A proximity effect bass boost is often used to enhance the low end, giving the voice greater authority. This works especially well on talent with high pitch voices.

Some speakers prefer to stand up, while some sit down. Generally, professional speakers that do drama readings stand up and work the mic. Nonprofessional speakers and talent that often refer to notes or the script may prefer to sit down. In this case, the microphone will be mounted on a table stand, or on a boom holding the mic over the table. In such a situation, problems with reflections from the table causing phase cancellations might be encountered. A directional mic, tilted up from the table, could help solve this problem.

Another nuisance is the rustling of papers on the table. The speaker may have to be worked with to keep this noise down. One way to work with them is to record the dialog in segments, so each segment can be laid out on the table and read without movement. At the end of each

segment, the papers can be rearranged for the next segment and recording started again.

Several techniques exist for recording more than one speaker. These include:

- Using a bidirectional mic with a speaker placed on each side. The distance of each speaker from the mic can be adjusted to balance the relative levels.
- Directional mics can be used, with the pattern for each mic being arranged to reject the other vocal talent. Each voice can then be routed to its own track, or combined together at the console.
- An omni mic or a cardioid mic pointed straight up in the middle of the speakers' circle can be used to pickup a group of speakers that are standing around it.
- Boundary mics are also effective for pickup of groups of speakers sitting around a table. The distance from each speaker to the boundary mic should generally be no greater than about three feet. If there are too many speakers to maintain this distance with one mic, more than one should be used.
- Lavaliere or clip-on mics can be used: these may be either wired or wireless. Typically, such a mic is placed below the speaker's chin, and sometimes is concealed within clothing. These mics often are designed with a low-frequency boost to compensate for the severe off-axis placement. Keep in mind that not all lavaliere mics are created equal: some sound great while others sound tinny. In addition, the sound level reaching a lavaliere or clip-on mic usually is much lower in level than a stand mic, therefore, greater amplification may be required.

Don't be afraid to experiment with the speaker, microphone type, windscreen and pop filter, or even the recording environment and mic distance, in order to achieve the best balance of presence, intelligibility, and noise reduction.

6 Stereo Miking Techniques

Chapter

Stereo Hearing

Before we investigate the basics of stereo microphone techniques, it helps to understand the ways that our ears are able to localize and perceive the direction of sound. One ear isn't able to discern the direction from which a sound originates; however, two ears can, via a process called binaural localization. This process works by using three cues that are received by the ears:

1. Interaural intensity differences
2. Interaural arrival-time differences
3. The effects of the pinna (outer ears)

Because the head casts an acoustic shadow to direct sound waves, middle- to higher-frequency sounds that originate from the right side reach the right ear at a higher intensity level than the left ear, causing an interaural intensity difference. Only sounds that are reflected from surrounding surfaces will reach the left ear (Figure 6-1). Since the reflected sound travels further and loses energy at each reflection, the intensity of sound that's perceived by the left ear is reduced, resulting in the signal being perceived as originating from the right.

This effect is relatively insignificant at lower frequencies, because the wavelengths are large compared to the diameter of the head and can easily bend around it. Thus, at lower frequencies a different method of localization,

known as interaural arrival-time differences, occurs. These time differences happen because the acoustic path to the left ear is slightly longer than that to the right ear. Thus, the left ear will sense the sound at a later time than the right ear (Figure 6-2). This method of localization, in combination with interaural intensity differences, lets us locate sounds that originate laterally over the entire frequency spectrum.

These intensity and delay cues let us perceive the angle from which a sound originates, but not whether the sound comes from the front, behind, or below. These final pieces of information are supplied by the pinna, which reflects incident sound into the ear via two ridges (Figure 6-3). These ridges introduce delays between the direct sound (which reaches the entrance of the ear canal) and the sound that's reflected from the ridges (which vary according to the source location).

It's interesting to note that beyond about 130° from the front axis there can be no reflections from the outer ridge because:

1. It's blocked by the pinna. Unreflected sounds are therefore delayed by 0–80 ms and are perceived as originating from the rear.
2. The inner ridge produces delays between 100 and 330 ms that help us perceive sources in the vertical plane. The delayed reflections from both ridges combine with the direct sound to produce frequency response colorations which are decoded by the brain

Figure 6-1
Interaural Intensity Differences

"Because the head casts an acoustic shadow to direct sound waves, middle- to higher-frequency sounds that originate from the right side reach the right ear at a higher intensity level than the left ear, causing an interaural intensity difference. Only sounds that are reflected from surrounding surfaces will reach the left ear. Since the reflected sound travels further and loses energy at each reflection, the intensity of sound that's perceived by the left ear is reduced, resulting in the signal being perceived as originating from the right."

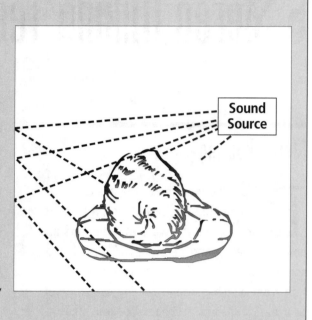

to help us locate sounds.

Small movements of the head provide additional position information, due to the changing source perspective. This last cue, however, is minor when compared to the other localization cues.

If there aren't any differences between what the left and right ear hears, the brain as-

Figure 6-2
Interaural Arrival Time Differences

"...at lower frequencies a different method of localization, known as interaural arrival-time differences, occurs. These time differences happen because the acoustic path to the left ear is slightly longer than that to the right ear."

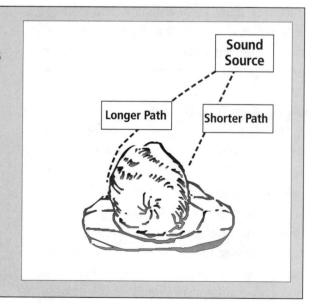

Figure 6-3
Pinna and Its Reflective Ridges

"It's interesting to note that beyond about 130° from the front axis there can be no reflections from the outer ridge because:

1. It's blocked by the pinna. Unreflected sounds are therefore delayed by 0–80 ms and are perceived as originating from the rear.
2. The inner ridge produces delays between 100 and 330 ms that help us perceive sources in the vertical plane. The delayed reflections from both ridges combine with the direct sound to produce frequency response colorations which are decoded by the brain to help us locate sounds."

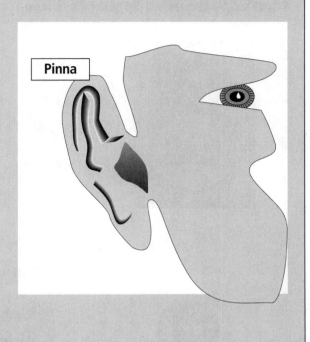

Pinna

sumes that the source is the same distance from each ear. Thus, if the same signal is fed to both speakers, the brain receives the sound identically in both ears and deduces that the source must originate from directly in front of the listener. By changing the proportions fed to the two loudspeakers, the engineer changes the interchannel intensity differences and thus creates the illusion that the sound source is positioned at any desirable point between the two or more speakers (Figure 6-4).

When to Use Stereo Miking

While stereo miking is often a reliable solution for recording ensembles and soloists in a live setting, there are also times when it can be used with great success in multitrack recording and overdubbing situations.

Stereo works well in capturing the tonality and spaciousness of many acoustic instruments, such as guitar, piano, banjo, drum kits, hammer dulcimers, marimbas, choruses, and backup vocals. In fact, nearly any instrument or sound source has an improved sense of spaciousness and presence when recorded using a stereo pair. There are a few exceptions which often mic better in mono, like upright acoustic bass, and instruments with tight sound radiating patterns, namely, horns, electric guitars, flutes, and other woodwinds. However, this is just an opinion: feel free to experiment and find out for yourself.

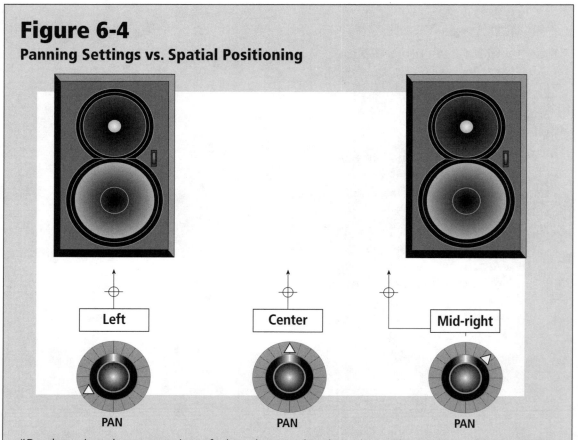

Figure 6-4
Panning Settings vs. Spatial Positioning

Left	Center	Mid-right
PAN	PAN	PAN

"By changing the proportions fed to the two loudspeakers, the engineer changes the interchannel intensity differences and thus creates the illusion that the sound source is positioned at any desirable point between the two or more speakers."

The concept of using stereo miking techniques to convey a sense of direction isn't new. In 1931, the British scientist Alan Dower Blumlein filed for his historic British Patent No. 394,325, in which he listed seventy claims, over twenty-two pages, regarding two channel stereo for disc recording and motion pictures. In his patent application, Blumlein stated:

"The fundamental object of the invention is to provide a sound recording, reproduction and/or transmission system whereby there is conveyed to the listener a realistic impression that the intelligence is being communicated to him over two acoustic paths in the same manner as he experiences in listening to everyday acoustic intercourse and this object embraces also the idea of conveying to the listener a true directional impression and thus, in the case in which the sound is associated with picture effects, improving the illusion that the sound is coming, and is only coming, from the artist or other sound source presented to the eye."

When speaking of stereo miking techniques, we're generally referring to the use of a two-microphone arrangement to attain a stereophonic image. This is different from the single-mic pickup, where stereo is created at the console through the use of panning and effects techniques.

Stereo miking techniques can be used, with equal effectiveness, in a close-mic situation, where a single instrument is recorded at close range in a multitrack studio or on-location environment, or for use in the distant overall miking of an instrument or ensemble: the only true limit is your imagination. There are four basic ways to create a stereo image with two microphones:

1. The spaced technique
2. The coincident technique
3. The near-coincident technique
4. The binaural technique.

Spaced Microphone Techniques

Spaced mic techniques were among the first that were used to relay a stereo image. Generally, this method uses two or more matched mics that are set symmetrically along a centerline that's perpendicular to the front plane of the sound source. The polar pattern of this stereo pair, their spacing, and their distance from the sound source are all variable. The stereo information in these configurations is created using differences in sound wave amplitude and arrival time, and can change radically as the distance to the sound source varies (Figure 6-5).

When using spaced microphone configurations, pay special attention to these potential problems:

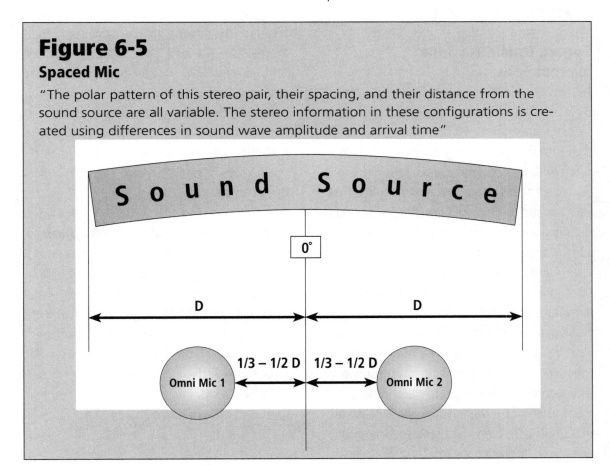

Figure 6-5
Spaced Mic

"The polar pattern of this stereo pair, their spacing, and their distance from the sound source are all variable. The stereo information in these configurations is created using differences in sound wave amplitude and arrival time"

- Low-frequency comb-filter effects (selective variations in the pickup frequency response) over the soundfield, especially at the extreme left and right of the field
- Vague center imaging: instruments near the center can stray from their true L-R positioning during playback
- Erratic mono compatibility

In order to keep the phase integrity of our spaced mics intact, let's refer back to the 3:1 principle, which states that "for every unit of distance measured between the mic and its source, the distance between the spaced pair should be at least three times that unit of measure." Since this condition isn't always met, phase interference in mono reproduction sometimes occurs.

Spaced Omnidirectional Microphones

This style typically uses two, and sometimes three, spaced omnidirectional mics. Common spacings are from 2–10 feet on either side of the centerline. The spacing is determined by the width of the sound source and by the mic pair's distance from that source. A general rule is that each mic should be placed one-third to one-half the distance from the centerline to the outer edge of the sound stage.

A three spaced mic technique uses a center mic in addition to the two microphone array. This tends to fill in the hole-in-the-middle that can result from the wide spacing of the two outer mics; and it may also be used to tighten the center imaging of the configuration. Although some amazing recordings have been made using this technique, the phase problems that occur with three mics tend to be sonically damaging, increasing the effects of comb-filter-

ing and raising the affected frequencies into the more noticeable mid and upper ranges of the spectrum.

Spaced Cardioid Microphones

The spaced cardioid method is similar to the above. However, since these mics are directional, they tend to favor the direct on-axis sound. Although this technique reduces unwanted reverb and room noises, coloration in the off-axis pickup of reverb, applause, etc. can occur. For this reason, orientation and placement is sometimes more critical than with omnidirectional mics.

Spaced Bidirectional Microphones

The rear lobe of the bidirectional mic, which provides the reverberation and audience response component, has the same sonic characteristics as the front lobe (i.e., there'll be little off-axis coloration). This method tends to have more reach to the front than the spaced cardioid pair, but has an equal reach in the rear. For this reason, the bidirectional pair can be placed further from the sound source than either an omni or cardioid pair to achieve the same degree of coverage.

Spaced Hypercardioid Microphones

Spaced hypercardioids use a polar pattern that's midway between the spaced cardioid and bidirectional techniques. The front lobe of the pickup is narrower than that of the cardioid while the small rear lobe has the reverse polarity qualities of the bidirectional. This polar response has the advantage—and in certain situations, disadvantage—of picking up the least room and off-axis sound.

Spaced Boundary Microphones

The spaced boundary pair is similar to the spaced omnidirectional pair, except that the polar pattern is hemispherical about the boundary surface.

Spaced Microphone Technique with Accent Mics

An accent microphone is often added to the basic two or three mic technique in order to emphasize a soloist within the overall sound-field image. Although more than one accent mic can be used, it's important to keep in mind that the main stereo pair is providing the basic overall coverage.

When using an accent microphone, choose your mic placement and the amount that the pickup is blended into the overall mix with care. Quite simply, it shouldn't discolor or change the balance of soloist to the other surrounding instruments within the stereo perspective. Good accent mic technique only adds presence to the sound of a solo passage and shouldn't be perceived as a separate pickup. In addition, careful and appropriate panning of an accent mic into the overall stereo image helps eliminate any wandering images that might occur with changes in solo intensity.

Coincident Microphone (X-Y) Technique

The coincident stereo technique uses a matched pair of directional mics that are offset with respect to each other along a horizontal plane. The angles formed by the microphone pair are typically symmetrical about the centerline of the sound source, such that the intensity of the sound being received at the outer edges of the soundfield are on axis with respect to one

marimba

Given that the mic diaphragms are spaced very closely together—as close as possible, without touching—there's little or no phase differences between the two capsules. Almost any polar pattern can be chosen, from sub-omni to bidirectional, depending on the technique and amount of pickup you want to be included.

Cardioid patterns are typically used in coincident stereo miking and are often placed at an included angle that ranges from 90–135°, at various distances ranging from distant to close, depending upon the amount of ambience or room sounds that you want to include. Often, the mic's outer axes are aimed near the extremes of the sound source. In some circumstances, an included angle as wide as 140–160° can be used.

A hypercardioid X-Y pair is similar to the cardioid pair, except that the included angle is typically narrower in order to preserve a solid center image. The increased reach of the hypercardioid lets you exclude more of the surrounding ambience, or lets you place the mics further back from the source. As a note, the small reverse-polarity lobes make this pattern a good compromise between the cardioid and the Blumlein X-Y technique.

In addition to using two matched mics as a stereo pair, coincident microphone systems that are specifically designed for this purpose are also currently available. Their design includes two coincident mic capsules that are mounted in a single case housing. With such a stereo mic, you can rotate the upper element 180°, relative to the lower element. This lets you offset the two capsules at any possible angle offset. In addition, many of the more expensive mics let you control the polar pattern of each pickup—

Figure 6-6
Coincident Mic

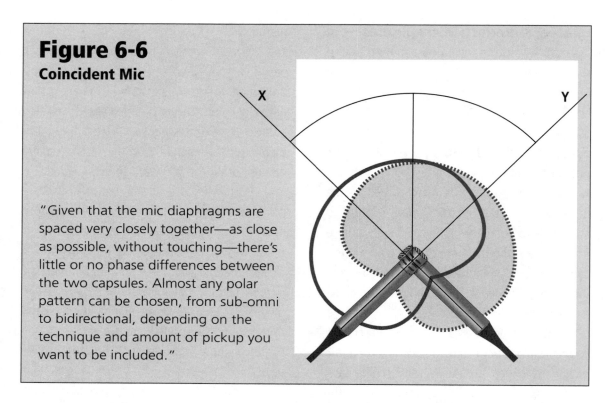

"Given that the mic diaphragms are spaced very closely together—as close as possible, without touching—there's little or no phase differences between the two capsules. Almost any polar pattern can be chosen, from sub-omni to bidirectional, depending on the technique and amount of pickup you want to be included."

either remotely or at the mic itself (Figure 6-7).

Blumlein X-Y Technique

The Blumlein (crossed figure eight) pair uses two bidirectional mics that are oriented at an included offset angle of 90°. The left quadrant and it's rear lobe are routed to the left channel while the opposing right quadrant and it's rear lobe are routed to the right (Figure 6-8).

As you can see, the benefit of this technique is that the rear quadrant combines with the front quadrant in the stereo cross-channeled image to pickup the entire lateral 360° soundfield image. In short, this technique produces a very natural sound: it's excellent in capturing the overall reverberant character of a room or hall—no matter how big or small.

Omnidirectional X-Y Technique

The technique of incorporating omnidirectional microphones into coincident X-Y stereo is used for close and semi close pickups. Since most omni mics tend to exhibit a degree of directionality at higher frequencies, configuring an omni pair at an included angle of 60–90° provides a stable and coherent center image, combined with a subtle sense of stereo space. Furthermore, there's little sense of image shift as the soloist moves—as can be the case with directional mics. The use of pressure (omni) capsules can eliminate the proximity effect and breath blasting problems that are associated with the pressure-gradient (directional) microphone pair.

MS Technique

The MS, or mid-side, stereo miking technique is similar to the X-Y method in that it uses two microphone capsules in close proximity. This may take the form of two coincident microphones or a single stereo mic that has been switched into the MS stereo mode (Figure 6-9).

In the classic MS configuration, one of the microphone capsules is designated to be the mid position microphone and is generally selected to have a cardioid pickup pattern that's oriented toward the sound source. The side capsule is generally given a figure-eight pattern that's oriented 90° laterally, facing to each side of the mid pickup.

Direct sound is picked up by the mid (M) capsule, while ambient and reverberant sound is picked up by the side (S) capsule. These outputs are then processed by a sum-and-difference matrix network that can resolve them into a conventional X-Y stereo signal: (M + S) and (M - S).

One major advantage of this system is its absolute monaural compatibility. When the left and right signals are combined, the sum will be solely the output from the mid pickup component ([M + S] + [M - S] = 2M) which contains the direct sound information. Since it's generally better that there be less reverberation in a mono signal than in a stereo signal, there's a built-in advantage to this technique.

MS stereo production's greatest claim to fame is the control that it offers over the stereo image during both production and post-production. Using MS, it's possible to adjust the ratio of mid-to-side information that's delivered to the sum-and-difference matrix at the audio production mixer or console. This lets you have remote control over the direct vs. ambient and stereo width information. It's equally possible to record the mid information on one track of a recorder or hard disk editor and the side

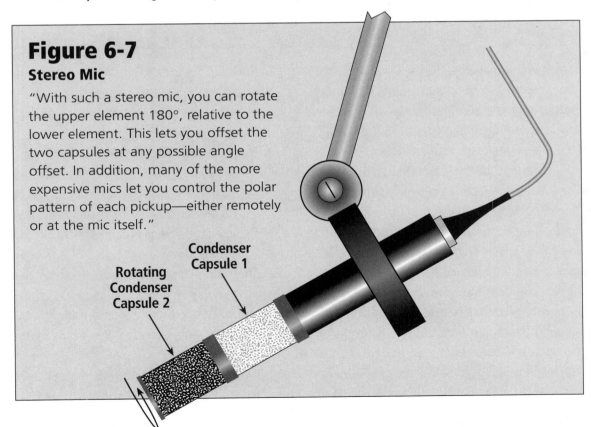

Figure 6-7
Stereo Mic

"With such a stereo mic, you can rotate the upper element 180°, relative to the lower element. This lets you offset the two capsules at any possible angle offset. In addition, many of the more expensive mics let you control the polar pattern of each pickup—either remotely or at the mic itself."

Condenser Capsule 1

Rotating Condenser Capsule 2

Figure 6-8
Blumlein X-Y Crossed Pair

"…this technique produces a very natural sound: it's excellent in capturing the overall reverberant character of a room or hall—no matter how big or small."

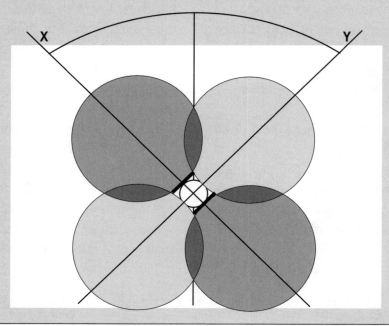

information on another. This lets you remix the data into an X-Y compatible signal during the mixdown phase, allowing you to make important decisions regarding stereo width and depth at a later and more controlled date.

Sum and difference matrix systems that use an active combining circuit or software for decoding MS stereo from a cardioid and a bidirectional microphone are commercially available. These systems adjust the matrix's mid-to-side ratio, either at a console line level insert point or in the software domain.

MS decoding is also accomplished by splitting the output from the side bidirectional mic with a Y cable built with the two output connections (inputs to board) out of phase with each other (Figure 6-10). Here's how you do it:

1. Hook up the bidirectional mic (side) to the phase inverting Y cable as shown above and plug the Y outputs (left and right) into two channels of the mixing board.

2. Plug a cardioid mic (mid) into another channel and center pan it. Pan the side mic channels to the center first and adjust the gain on each side mic channel until you get a null. Then pan the side mic channels hard left and right, accordingly.

3. Bring up the mid mic to about the same gain as the side mic (using only this channel will give you a good, mono sound). Adding in the side channels increases the width of the stereo spread.

4. If you use reverb, add it to just the mid channel, as a send from both side channels will

Figure 6-9
MS Stereo Miking

"In the classic MS configuration, one of the microphone capsules is designated to be the mid position microphone and is generally selected to have a cardioid pickup pattern that's oriented toward the sound source. The side capsule is generally given a figure-eight pattern that's oriented 90° laterally, facing to each side of the mid pickup."

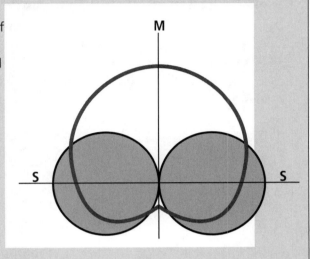

be out of phase and will cancel.

Binaural Techniques

The binaural technique is intended specifically for playback via headphones. It's often configured to use two omnidirectional mics that are placed into the ears of a dummy head to simulate the sound that's received by an actual listener at that position. This technique can be extremely realistic, and can accurately give you localization and movement clues of sounds coming from both the horizontal and vertical planes. Unfortunately, these characteristic illusions don't reproduce well—if at all—over

Figure 6-10
MS Y Cable For Splitting the Side Mic

"MS decoding is also accomplished by splitting the output from the side bidirectional mic with a Y cable built with the two output connections (inputs to board) out of phase with each other."

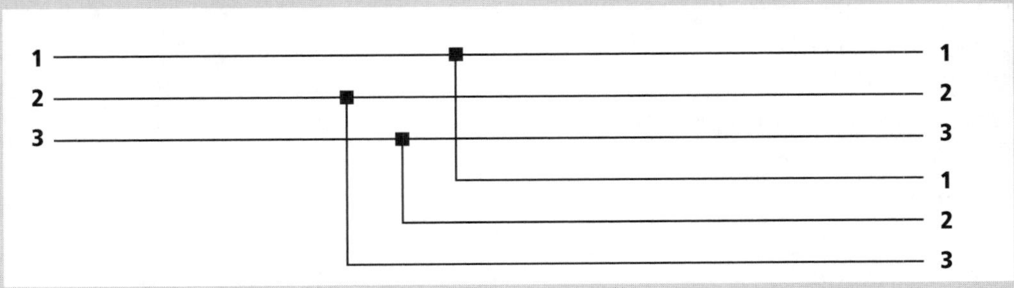

Figure 6-11

Simple Quasi-binaural Setup Configuration

"…techniques have been configured using two omnidirectional (or even bidirectional) mics that are placed approximately 3–4" on either side of a sound absorbing baffle. This simple approach may give you results that are similar to the dummy head system and can also give sufficient isolation between channels to allow for realistic stereo reproduction over speakers.

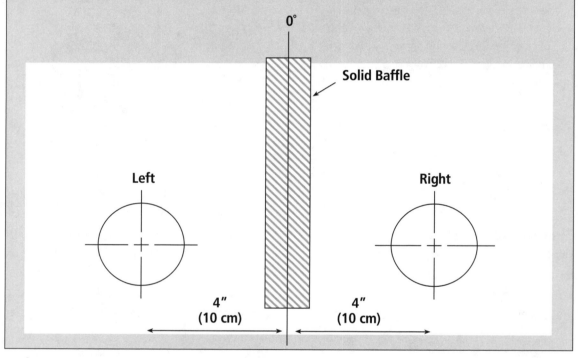

speakers.

Similar techniques have been configured using two omnidirectional (or even bidirectional) mics that are placed approximately 3–4 inches on either side of a sound absorbing baffle. This simple approach may give you results that are similar to the dummy head system and can also give sufficient isolation between channels to allow for realistic stereo reproduction over speakers (Figure 6-11).

Chapter 7 Outboard Stuff

Intro to Outboard Stuff

The term outboard stuff refers to electronics that are used in the recording chain after the mic has converted the acoustic sound waves into a corresponding electrical signal. So, why should we deal with this in a microphone manual? While the microphone is the primary link to the sound wave, what happens to the electrical signal that it generates is often nearly as important to getting the desired sound as the right mic and good techniques are.

After the electrical signal leaves the mic, it goes through a preamp to amplify the mic's low output to a voltage level that's easier to process with the rest of the recording equipment. Often, it then goes through an equalizer, compressor/limiter, gate, and reverb unit before the sound that comes out of the speakers feels right.

Sometimes this outboard stuff is used to create what the engineer and producer feel as being an accurate sound reproduction of the performance. Other times, it's used to create a totally different sound from what's being picked up by the mic. For example, if you're trying to recreate a special type of sound, you might need a number of signal processors and general "toys" to create it. Without them, getting just the right sound might be difficult or impossible.

Of course, this chapter isn't an exhaustive work on this subject, but is intended to give you an idea of why outboard stuff is important for getting certain types of sounds.

Microphone Preamps

In Chapter 2, we saw that most mics put out a relatively low signal voltage that must be amplified to line level in order to interface with a console and other standard studio electronics that are found in the recording chain. Such a mic preamp must be able to boost the mic's output by up to 60 dB or more. Truth is, this is a considerable amount of amplification—much more than all the electronics in the rest of the recording chain. For this reason, a mic preamp can often have a great effect on the overall sound reproduction. Therefore, to some people, the choice of preamp is an important decision in a session's gear selection process.

Many mic preamp types are available and none of them are going to sound the same, even when using the same mic and recording setup. Many engineers, producers, and musicians have their favorite mic preamps that they take from job to job. Studios often have several different preamps so the engineer can have his or her choice.

The most commonly encountered type of mic preamps are those that are built into a console, mixer, or recorder. These preamps range from terrible to quite good. The console manufacturer has to factor the cost of their integrated preamps into the price of the console and, if it's built to sell at a competitive price, less attention may be given to building a quality input section. However, before simply writing off the preamps that are built into the console, give them a good listen. Some of them are more than adequate for most recording jobs.

In recent times, there's been a lot of interest in stand-alone mic preamps, ranging from basic boxes that do an adequate job, to top-of-the-line preamps that have to be heard to be believed. Typically, great care has been put into the design and construction of these preamps as the competition isn't always in price, but rather in performance. Good stand-alone mic preamps typically come as one or two channel units and can be more expensive than a basic project studio mixer. Different designers and manufacturers have different concepts of the sound that a good mic preamp should have. At the very least, a good mic preamp must have the following characteristics:

- Low self-noise at high amplification levels—a signal to noise ratio of at least 90 dB
- Transparency
- Freedom from radio frequency (RF) interference
- Flat frequency response to 30 kHz or more and overall response to as high as 200 kHz with good square wave response

Some high quality preamps are fully solid-state with no input or output transformers while others use only vacuum tubes. Many use a hybrid of both solid-state and vacuum tube amplification devices. In addition, some use input and/or output transformers for interfacing with balanced mic and output lines while still others (in both solid-state and tube designs) use differential amplifiers, rather than transformers, to offer balanced inputs and outputs.

The choice of mic preamp is a matter of personal taste and the bottom line is—whatever works for you. There probably are nearly as many opinions on what mic preamp to use as there are engineers who use them. Here are some of the opinions and the basis cited for them:

- Engineers that record primarily popular music often use a mic preamp that can be overdriven to add distortion as a part of the sound. Often these preamps use input and output transformers.
- Engineers that record classical music generally use preamps that are transparent, simply amplifying the signal from the mic while contributing as little to the sound as possible; also, they typically have extended frequency response, low noise, and lots of headroom. These preamps often avoid using transformers for input and output. The ultra-clean mic preamps used in state-of-the-art recording are expensive, use high grade, hand selected and matched components, and are built with special care.

No matter what brand or type of high quality (i.e., expensive) outboard mic preamp you choose, it's almost certain that it'll give better results than the mic preamp that's built into many of today's mixers—and it most certainly will make a difference in the recorded sound.

Tube vs. Solid-state Preamps

There are numerous differences that are claimed by makers of tube and solid-state mic preamps, and probably as many opinions as to which work best and why, as there are engineers. The truth is, the simple fact that one preamp uses tubes for amplification and another uses transistors is no indication of quality or sound. Beyond the fact that tube and solid-state devices have different overload characteristics—which may add or detract from the desired sound—both types are used in the most critical of recording situations.

Some engineers and producers claim that tube preamps have more bass, cleaner midrange and a more accurate sound than solid-state preamps, and that solid-state preamps lack air and have too much sibilance emphasis. Other engineers feel that solid-state preamps do the best job for them. In the end, the choice of whether to use a tube, solid-state, or hybrid design preamp is entirely up to you.

Overload and Its Effects

A mic preamp, be it tube, solid-state or hybrid, can be driven into overload. Too much signal from the mic, or at some point in the amplification circuit, will exceed the ability of a tube or transistor to operate linearly and will cause it to clip—resulting in a distorted sound. Clipping can be prevented by either inserting a pad at the mic or by reducing the preamp's trim to a level that's easier to handle.

In severe cases, overloads and clipping distortion can make the sound unlistenable—unless that's the sound you want. Slight overloads are sometimes difficult to recognize and may show up simply as a momentary harshness in the sound. It's often difficult for this problem to be corrected once the track's been recorded. However, some digital editors can reduce or correct momentary distortions. Therefore, it's worthwhile to spend some time experimenting with, creating, and listening to slight overload distor-

tion to be able to recognize it during an actual session. Setting up the input gain to keep the levels below distortion with the performer playing at their loudest helps minimize overload; but, once the record button is pushed, performers often get into the music and exceed these maximum levels. For this reason, it's a good idea to set the input trim a little low to give more headroom than you feel is necessary, rather than to risk distortion.

A slight amount of overload can add an effect to a sound. Overloading a tube circuit often produces even harmonic distortion. This is the emphasis of the 2nd, 4th, and 6th harmonics. This type of harmonic distortion is perceived by the ear as adding a fullness and body to the sound and is often introduced to an otherwise clean signal to fool the ear into hearing the sound as being clearer and more pleasant. Even the heavily distorted sound from an overloaded tube guitar amp can be perceived as being pleasant and, in fact, has become a part of its signature sound.

Solid-state devices, on the other hand, tend to emphasize odd harmonics when overloaded: 3rd, 5th, 7th and so on. Odd harmonics are generally perceived by the ear as adding harshness to the sound. For example, strong 3rd and 5th harmonic distortion can make a sound somewhat metallic while 7th and higher odd harmonics result in an edgy quality that has a sharp attack.

Transformers vs. Transformerless Input/Output

The function of a professional mic preamp is to amplify one or more balanced, low impedance microphones to provide a line level output that is transparent, flat, and low in noise over the entire audio spectrum. Interface between the mic, the preamp, and the outside line level world is handled through either a transformer or a transformerless differential amplifier circuit. Of course, there are often strong differences of opinion among recording engineers as to which type to use. Again, it's useful to understand the differences between them.

A mic preamp's input transformer is made up of two separate coils of wire that are wound around a metal core. The primary winding is designed to match the impedance and balanced configuration of the mic. The output winding is designed to match and interface with the preamp's electronics.

Transformers, by their nature, have a limited frequency bandwidth of at least 20 Hz to 20 kHz. The fact that transformers will only pass a limited frequency range can be both a benefit and a problem. It can eliminate low- and high-end interference by simply not passing it. On the other hand, transformers can have their own sound by introducing a mild form of distortion that's known as ringing. This ringing can interfere with the signal's overall clarity if careful, and sometimes expensive, design steps aren't taken. It should also be said that sometimes this side effect could benefit a preamp's sound and character.

Transformerless designs are much less expensive to build and don't have the problems of ringing that are associated with their cousin. Their overall transient response and frequency response is also greatly improved.

As usual, keep in mind that the choice between the two is often simply a matter of personal preference, as all high quality preamps sound good whether or not they use transformers.

Signal Processors

Choosing the best mic, placement, and mic preamp won't necessarily guarantee that you'll get the sound you want. While the goal is to capture great sounds by using the right mic technique, this might not be possible due to problems with the recording environment, the performer, the nature of the sound being recorded, or simply the fact that the style of the music requires further treatment to get the right production feel.

This section deals with outboard devices and their usage for shaping a performer's sound: these include compressor/limiters, equalizers, gates, and reverb units. The discussion is intended to give only a basic intro to how these devices are used, what they do, and some typical settings for commonly encountered applications. Even if you feel that you'll never use any of these devices, it's well worth taking the time to get a basic understanding of them. When used properly, these processing "toys" can help solve problems, fill out or alter a track, and/or create a sound that can fit the project to a tee.

In practice, signal processors should be used as little as possible, and then only enough to come up with the sound you want. In order to give you the most flexibility, it's a good idea to record the signal straight from the mic without processing it until mixdown. It's nearly impossible to undo a processed track once it's been recorded. Sometimes, however, it makes sense to lay down a track with certain forms of processing, especially if you already know the effect you want. Just be careful!

As usual, the suggestions given in this

chapter are only starting places and clues for achieving a particular sound: there are no standards. As you set out on the road to processing heaven, keep a written log of the situation, where it was used and the effect and settings you used. You could even write your own reference manual of settings that work for you. Above all, keep experimenting until you get the sounds that you want.

Compressor/Limiter

The compressor/limiter is a device that reduces the level of a signal by a set amount when it exceeds a preset threshold. At lower gain reduction settings, it serves to even out volume level differences that occur from note to note. At higher gain reduction settings, it can be used to prevent levels from going over the set threshold, thus acting as a limiter. This is useful to prevent peaks from overloading the recording chain.

Compressors are also used to decrease the dynamic range of the material and raise low level signals, so the overall recording sounds louder. Common uses include fattening drum sounds, evening out the note-to-note level differences of bass instruments, smoothing out vocals, increasing a guitar's sustain, and giving more prominence to selected instruments or vocalists in the mix.

As a caveat, compression always lessens the openness of the sound; therefore, the general rule is to use compression sparingly and only when needed as a tool for getting the sound you want.

Compressor Controls

Here's a listing of the most important controls on a typical compressor and what they do:

- **Threshold**—This control sets the level above which the gain of signals entering the compressor will be attenuated. It's calibrated in dB and typically ranges from about -40 dB to +20 dB. The compressor won't process any signal that falls below this threshold and will process all signals above it.

- **Ratio**—This sets the amount by which a signal exceeding the threshold will be attenuated at the compressor's output. Some compressors have a set of pre-selected ratios that can be set by a switch. Others have continuously variable ratios (1:1 to infinity) that are set by a rotary control. For example, if the ratio is set at 4:1, a signal exceeding the threshold by 4 dB will be increased at it's output by 1 dB. A ratio of 10:1 means that the level of a signal 10 dB above the threshold will increase by only 1 dB at the output. Whenever a compression ratio of 10 or 12:1 is used, the type of processing is generally referred to as limiting.

- **Attack**—This setting, calibrated in milliseconds, determines how fast the compressor acts on a signal that exceeds the threshold. A fast attack time can sound unnatural; a slow attack time might sound more natural but might not prevent clipping. This setting should be experimented with to see if it's fast enough to let the compressor do its job, but not so fast as to color the sound.

- **Release**—This control, calibrated in milliseconds and seconds, determines how fast the compressor returns the signal to its original gain after it's fallen below the threshold. A fast release setting will cause the compressor to follow every level variation in the material and may be heard as an undesirable pumping effect and a decrease in the signal's dynamics. Longer release times provide a more natural sound, but hold the output level down for a longer time before releasing it back to its unprocessed level.

- **Automatic switch**—Many compressors have an "automatic" switch that disables the attack and release controls and lets the compressor's circuit automatically set the attack and release times by tracking the input signal and applying attack and release as needed. This mode often works best for compressing an overall mix.

- **Stereo coupling switch**—This switch is used on most two-channel compressors to couple the channels so that when compression and release are sensed on one channel, the same processing will be applied to the other. This assures that both channels of a stereo mix will be treated the same and won't unnaturally wander from side to side.

- **Hard knee/Soft knee**—In hard knee mode, compression is applied rapidly with increased gain reduction. This mode doesn't necessarily give you natural results, but it can be useful on instruments, like drums, where a lot of gain reduction is needed fast. In the soft knee mode, compression is applied more gradually, resulting in a smoother, more natural sound. Soft knee compression works best for non-percussive instruments such as basses, guitars, and vocals. Many compressors with this feature don't have a separate switch, but apply soft knee or hard knee compression automatically depending on the compression ratio, the selected threshold, and the input signal.

- **Output control**—This control adjusts the compressor's output level and is used to raise the overall gain that may have been reduced during compression, or simply to help you match levels with the next device in the chain.

Compressor Settings

The following setting suggestions are given only as examples of control settings that often work for getting a good sound from a compressor. They're simply a place to start and aren't a substitute for your own experimentation. The threshold setting depends on the level of the signal that's going to the compressor and must be adjusted on a case by case basis to get the best effect.

- **Bass**—The note volumes of acoustic and electric basses are often uneven from note to note. Without compression, some notes may seem simply to drop out, losing punch and clarity—even with the most studied mic technique. Typical starting settings are: Ratio: 4:1–12:1 (around 5:1 often does the job on an acoustic bass); Attack: Slow, up to 50 milliseconds for acoustic bass. Try a faster attack (8–20 milliseconds) for electric bass; Release: 0.25–0.5 seconds; soft knee type.

  Drum sounds can be changed a lot by using compression. High compression ratios and long release times lengthen the time of the hit, whereas fast attack times can cause too much pumping and make the set sound unnatural. Starting drum settings:

- **Kick**—Attack: 10 milliseconds or longer; Release: 175–225 milliseconds; Ratio: 4:1 to 8:1.

- **Snare**—Attack: 5–10 milliseconds; Release: 150 milliseconds; Ratio: 4:1–6:1.

- **Toms**—Basically, start same as snare.

- **Acoustic guitar**—Attack: 15–25 milliseconds; Release: 0.5 second; Ratio: 4:1–8:1.
- **Electric guitar**—Attack: 10–50 milliseconds; Release: 0.4–0.6 second; Ratio: 4:1–8:1.
- **Vocals**—Attack: fast as possible; Release—0.5 second; Ratio: 4:1–8:1.
- **Mix**—Use automatic mode, if available, and switch the stereo coupling switch in. If there's no automatic mode, Attack: 10 milliseconds; Release: 0.5 second; Ratio: 2:1–6:1.

Gate

A gate is a device that cuts off the sound below a user-set threshold. When the signal level falls below this level, it simply cuts off. Gates are useful for cutting the signal from an open mic that's not being used, and in eliminating unwanted noise from leakage or tape hiss during mixdown.

Gates have to be handled carefully to avoid noticeable glitches or premature cutoffs on dynamic program material. They're extremely useful for adding punch and separation to drum tracks and for tightening up bass tracks.

Controls

The threshold control, which is calibrated in dB, determines the level below which a signal will be processed. The attack control, which is calibrated in milliseconds, determines how fast the gating action starts after the signal falls below the threshold. The hold function, which is calibrated in seconds, extends the release time to avoid triggering the gate repeatedly during short pauses, which can be heard as an unwanted artifact: longer hold times are good

for speech recording. Release, which is calibrated in seconds, sets how long it takes to restore the signal to its normal gain after gating; it should be adjusted to preserve the natural fade out of the instrument. Ratio determines the change in output level relative to input level. At low ratio settings, the gate acts like a downward expander that has a high ratio (usually around 30:1). Range, which is calibrated in dB, determines the amount by which the signal falling below the threshold will be attenuated. Range settings from 10 dB to 20 dB will generally let the gate do its job while keeping the effects of the gating unnoticeable.

Some Suggested Settings

The following setting suggestions are given only as examples of control settings that often work for getting a good sound from a gate. They're simply a place to start, and aren't a substitute for your own experimentation.

- **Bass**—Basses, especially acoustic ones, have a fairly long sustain, and a note can reverberate for some time after being played. Gating the bass mic to cut off this sustain and reverberation can add considerable clarity and punch. The trick is to set the gate so there's enough sustain to give the bass its characteristic sound without chopping off the note's ring. If the threshold is set too high, the attack too slow, and the release is too long, the gate will cut off the start of the next note. Try starting with the threshold set at around -30 dB, and adjust upward as needed to get a punchy bass sound that doesn't constantly trigger the gate. Set the attack fairly fast: 2–6 milliseconds. Set the release at around 0.4–0.5 second. Set hold at the lowest setting; set ratio at 30:1. Set range at about 30 dB. Then, listen carefully and adjust each parameter to get the clarity and punchiness you want.

- **Drums**—Gating a drum mic can prevent it from picking up leakage when it isn't being played. When properly used in conjunction with good close-miking techniques, this can clean up the drum sound considerably, help reduce phase cancellation and comb filter effects. In addition, it'll add a lot of punch to the overall drum mix.

- **Snare**—Each drum mic might (or might not) need to be individually gated. If only one drum can be gated, however, gate the snare drum mic as it generally picks up more of every other drum in the kit. Start with the threshold at 0; attack and release at the fastest settings available; hold at the shortest period available; range at the lowest setting, and ratio at 30:1. Work from there for settings that open the gate in time to get the clean percussive attack of the hit, with sufficient tail off sustain to preserve the drum's characteristics—so there's no noticeable pumping. Snare and other very percussive drums require a fast release, whereas release times may be longer for cymbals and toms, and much longer for kick drums. Be aware of the pickup pattern of each mic and adjust them so the patterns exclude as much sound as possible from the other instruments. Too much high-end, off-axis pickup from cymbals and hi-hat, for example, can make it hard to properly gate the adjacent snares and toms.

- **Controlling sound leakage**—Start with low threshold levels, around -30 dB or more, to pass the signal without gating. Then, raise the threshold just enough to suppress the unwanted leakage without also cutting out the attack of the instrumentalist or vocalist. Slower release times generally work better with singers.

Equalization

Equalization selectively changes the relative level of frequencies over the audio spectrum. While the goal is to avoid the use of equalization by proper mic selection and technique, using EQ carefully can help fine tune a recording or recorded track, altering the sound for a desired effect.

Equalization can be an extremely useful tool, compensating for frequency response and problems with the recording space, mic, and sometimes with the tonalities of an instrument or vocalist. As with all signal processing, the best rule is to use as little as possible to do the job. You may have heard the age-old saying, "We can fix it in the mix!" Basically, the use of EQ as a crutch or Band-Aid to correct for inadequacies or problems in the originally recorded sound is at best a compromise to getting the best sound possible onto tape. If it's at all possible, take the time to choose the right mic, placement, and sound to get the job done right. You and the listening public will be glad you did.

It's a basic fact that every engineer has his or her own approach to equalization, and every recording situation requires an original approach. The following discussion is only a guide to help you to understand how equalization can be used in conjunction with good mic techniques to get the best recorded sound.

Equalizer Principles and Types

All equalizers have one or more controls for boosting or cutting a specified frequency called the "center" frequency. This cutting or boosting generally affects frequencies on each side of this point, with the number of affected frequencies being determined by the bandwidth. The narrower the bandwidth, the fewer affected frequencies around the center point.

Graphic Equalizers

Graphic equalizers divide the music frequency spectrum into bands where the center frequencies that are affected by the boost/cut controls are predetermined and generally are spaced to match musical intervals (such as an octave or 1/3 of an octave). These equalizers are easily recognized by a series of slider controls.

Parametric Equalizers

Parametric equalizers have fewer bands; usually three or four, with the center frequencies of each band being adjustable. In addition, most modern-day parametric equalizers let you adjust the bandwidth around the affected center frequency. Another related type is the selectable frequency equalizer, which has a set, predetermined number of center frequencies and a predetermined bandwidth. This is the type most often found on mixers which have a three band equalizer section, simply labeled "low," "mid," and "high."

Some consoles and mixers have more options: In addition to a "low" and "high" control, they often include a "low mid" and "high mid" control that has parametric frequencies and possibly Q, as well. This and other equalizer types can also be found on many outboard mic preamps.

Equalizer Settings

This section will delve into equalizer settings and their effect on an instrument, vocal or mix. It's intended to give you starting-point guidelines for getting desirable sounds when the sound from the mic simply isn't delivering—even when using good technique. Again, equalization is a tool that can enhance the sound; however, it's not a substitute for good mic techniques and should be used sparingly.

In general, an equalizer can be used, to some extent, to control notes that are louder than the rest due to instrument or room resonance. If room resonance is a problem, this is better controlled with mic placement and room baffling techniques (See Chapter 3.) If an instrument has a note that stands out and can't be tamed by adjusting the instrument, it might be necessary to search out the offending frequency with a parametric equalizer and adjust it into balance with the rest.

As a basic guideline, it's generally better to cut than to boost. A small cut in the high end can sound like a boost in the lows. It's also often best to record without equalization and apply it during mixdown.

Each frequency range has its own characteristic sound:

- The very low end, 100 Hz and lower, is warm.
- Boominess generally occurs around 200 Hz.
- The low-mid area, from around 250–1,000 Hz, adds depth and body.
- From above 1 kHz to about 2 kHz, a boost may produce a more tinny and nasal sound.
- The range from 2–4 kHz is the presence range and can bring a sound out of the mix, mak-

ing it sound warmer.

- Above 5 kHz affects the areas where harshness is most often heard. However, cymbals are clear up in the 8–10 kHz range: some engineers boost frequencies clear up to 17 kHz to add air.

Applying Equalization

- **Bass**—Watch out for overly boosting the low end. Often it's better to cut the very low end to clean up the sound, edging it back in until the warmth returns. A boost between 100 and 200 Hz can add body to a weak bass sound. You can boost a little between 500 and 800 Hz to get a raspy sound. Attack and punch comes from the region of about 700–1000 Hz; a boost in this area can help fill out thin sounds. Upper midrange boost at 2–5 kHz adds impact and an edge that can help the bass cut through on small speakers, while a cut in the 4–5 kHz range can help eliminate pick noise. If the bass and kick drum are hard to differentiate, try boosting the bass a little in the 60–70 Hz range and cutting the kick drum a little in this range.

Drum Tip

As a short note, jazz and small country and dance kits are treated differently from kits used in rock and pop; the differences in sound between these genres need to be taken into account during equalization.

- **Drums**—Equalization on drums depends on the sound you want to get, the kit you are recording, and the mic technique that's used. A low-end boost, in the range of 80–250 Hz, can add fullness. A cut in the low midrange from 300–500 Hz can help clean up the sound, while a moderate boost in the high end (around 5 kHz) can add crispness.

- **Kick**—Boost at the bottom end, 50–80 Hz for depth and a rounded sound. A few dB of boost at around 250 Hz can help give an impression of fullness. A cut of several dB in the 200–400 Hz ranges can improve clarity. A cut in the 400–600 Hz ranges helps provide a more open sound. Boosting in the 2.5 to as high as 10 kHz range brings out the beater sound and attack transients. Slap attack occurs around 2.5 kHz.

- **Snare**—Low-end boost in the 100–130 Hz ranges adds fullness. A little low-mid boost, around 250 Hz, adds warmth. Snap can be brought out with a boost in the 3–6 kHz ranges. A high-end boost around 8–10 kHz adds crispness and brings out the attack. High end cut helps create a warmer sound. If both a top and bottom mic are used, equalizing them differently can enhance the effect—especially for rock. Try cutting the low end substantially on the top mic: cut the midrange a few dB in the 800–1000 Hz range. Give a slight boost in the 1.2–1.5 kHz range and a few dB cut in the high end, around 9–10 kHz. On the bottom mic, cut the bass below about 250 Hz; cut substantially around 350–450 Hz and 750–850 Hz; cut slightly in the 3.5–4 kHz range; and boost the high end a little.

- **Toms**—Floor toms develop fullness at around 20–120 Hz: rack toms at around 240 Hz. A boost in these regions helps bring out the bottom end. Find attack emphasis in the 5 kHz region. A boost in the 4–8 kHz region can add presence, and a boost in the high end, 10 kHz or more, can add air.

- **Hi-hat**—The clank sound can be found around 200 Hz. As there's little below 150 Hz, substantial bass roll-off below this helps clean up the sound and minimize the effects of leakage from the drums. A boost around 10 kHz adds "sheen."

- **Cymbals**—Cymbals also develop their clank sound around 200 Hz. Cymbals actually don't produce much below about 1 kHz, except the clank. A low-mid boost—where the clank is preserved—and a cut in the low end and the upper midrange, can help clean up the sound and minimize leakage. Clankiness can be cleaned up with a cut in the 1–2 kHz region. The shimmer can be found in the 5–10 kHz region.

- **Overheads**—Roll off the low end, below 100 Hz, to clean up the sound. If you want to add more air or sheen, try boosting at 10 kHz or above.

- **Acoustic Guitar**—Try to get the best sound possible onto tape without any equalization. You can add equalization, if necessary, in the mix. The low end is in the 80–120 Hz range; body is around 250 Hz; and clarity and punch in the region of 2.5–5 kHz. Rolling off the bass below 80–100 Hz can clean up the sound and aid in getting rid of boominess without an apparent loss in bass. If boominess persists, try cutting at around 200 Hz. Boosting the lower midrange slightly can give an impression of having more bass without the boom. Boosting the upper midrange, around 2.5–5 kHz will give more punch. Boosting the upper midrange, up to around 7 kHz, can help with presence. To make a lead acoustic guitar stand out from a backup guitar, try equalizing the lead with a little more upper midrange boost: if the other guitar is given any upper mid boost, make it at a different frequency from the lead.

- **Electric Guitar**—The electric guitar develops fullness at around 240 Hz, and bite and presence are at around 2.5 kHz. Boominess from room resonance can be cleaned up with a cut at 100 Hz or less. Boosting the area of 125–250 Hz a few dB can add warmth. A more substantial boost at around 2.5–4 kHz might help bring out rhythm guitars and emphasize the attack, while a boost of 4–6 dB around 5 kHz helps with the lead, bringing out bite and presence. Above this range, there's usually not much to play with. To separate an electric guitar from an acoustic guitar, focus on a slight boost in the 250–350 Hz ranges for the electric, and the upper midrange for the acoustic.

- **Horns**—Horns develop their fullness in the 120–240 Hz range, and become shrill at around 5–7.5 kHz. A boost in the 300–400 Hz ranges helps fatten the sound. Too much emphasis in the 1–3.5 kHz range develops harshness, while a cut in this range helps tame harshness. If high-end boost is needed, apply it in the 6–10 kHz ranges.

- **Piano**—Low-end emphasis of a piano is in the range of 80–150 Hz. The bass can be fattened by a small boost in this range. Cut in the area between 250 and 350 Hz to reduce boom. The piano presence frequencies are between 2.5 and 5 kHz. Boosts in that range help bring out the attack, making the piano stand out from other instruments. A sharp narrow bandwidth boost at around 2.5 kHz produces a honky-tonk sound.

- **Violin**—The violin develops its fullness at around 250 Hz; a slight boost here can help. Harshness lies between 1 and 3.5 kHz. Scratchiness appears at around 7.5–10 kHz and a high-end cut might be necessary to get rid of it. The violin has overtones that go beyond this range, so don't cut the high end unless it's necessary to get rid of scratch—as when recording some fiddlers or young musicians that play on inferior instruments.

- **Vocals**—Vocals develop fullness around 120 Hz, boom at 200–250 Hz, presence around 5 kHz, and sibilance at 7.5–10 kHz. Avoid boosting the 1–2 kHz range; however, a boost in the midrange or mid-highs often helps vocals stand out. Lead vocals usually benefit from a few dB boost in the 2.5–3.5 kHz range, along with a similar boost in the high range, from 6–10 kHz (watch for sibilants). Backup vocals can be made to interfere less with the lead, and sound cleaner, by using a little low end cut, a few dB cut around the same mid-frequency where the lead vocal is boosted, and a slight high end boost.

- **Mix**—Equalization of the entire mix is usually (but not always) left to mastering operations, rather than initial recording and mixing. Overall equalization can affect the stereo imaging and positioning of the instruments or vocalists. Be aware of the effect that EQ can have on individual instruments and vocalists in the mix. Too much boosting in the same frequency range of several tracks can result in an unwanted buildup at this frequency range. After a track is equalized to sound right, listen to it in the mix to be sure it works with the other tracks. To move a sound back in the mix, try rolling off its top end. To separate instruments, equalize them differently.

Reverb

Adding reverb to tracks that were recorded dry is an age-old practice. Reverb can be used as an important tool to improve listenability, or it can be used in an exaggerated fashion to achieve an effect. Different types of reverb devices have been developed over the years, each having their own unique sound. The fundamental types are acoustic echo chamber, plate, spring, and contemporary digital reverb units. Besides adding naturalness and a room sound to the recording, increasing the reverb time on a particular instrument can have the effect of moving it back farther in the mix. There are no hard, fast rules about adding reverb: your ear will have to be the judge. However, it's often best to judge on the "less is more" side—unless you really want an exaggerated reverb effect.

Bass instruments, like basses and kick drums, generally shouldn't have reverb added to them. If any reverb is used, the reverb time should be kept short and the low frequencies should be equalized out. On drums, a plate reverb setting often is used, with a reverb time of 1–2.5 seconds and predelay of 20–25 milliseconds. For guitar, small room or plate settings often are used, with a reverb time of 1–4 seconds and a predelay of 15–50 milliseconds: too much reverb on a guitar can muddy up the sound. On violins, try a plate or small hall set for 1–2.5 seconds reverb time with a predelay of 20–80 milliseconds. On piano, try a large hall setting with 2–4 seconds reverb time and a predelay of up to 50 milliseconds. For vocals, try a small hall or plate simulation with a 1.5–4 second reverb time and a predelay of 20–70 milliseconds: a long delay time simulates doubling and can be used to fatten sounds.

That's all for now, the rest is up to you! As we said before: On the road to processing heaven, keep a written log of the situation, where it was used, and the effect and settings that you used. You could even write your own reference manual of settings that work for you. Above all, keep experimenting until you get the sounds that you want.

Chapter 8 The CD

The Compact Disc (CD) accompanying this book illustrates the miking techniques discussed in the book. The CD track illustrating each technique is identified in the text of the book where the particular technique is discussed. Generally, each track illustrates the most basic technique or techniques for each application, that will produce a commercially acceptable recording.

Wherever possible, we decided to use microphones and recording equipment that's readily available and in common use to produce these recordings. The performer, studio, mic, and facility used for each track is listed in the first track description for each instrument.

CD Track	Description

Track 1   Introduction to the CD

Track 2   The dynamic mic, Shure SM58. Vintage ribbon mic, RCA 44BX. Modern ribbon mic, Beyer M160. The condenser mic, AKG C3000.

Track 3   Proximity effect, RCA 44BX.

Track 4   Comparison between dynamic (Shure SM58, vintage ribbon (RCA, 44BX), modern ribbon (Beyer M160), and condenser (AKG C3000) with wood block, maracas, triangle.

Track 5   Accordion, Mic 1 has one mic 6" off end of right side of the accordion, with another placed 6" off left side, panned to "tight" stereo, Calrec 2050 cardioids. (Terry Wergeland, Robert Lang Studio)

Accordion, Mic 2, 12" in front of center of bellows, Calrec 2050 cardioid.

Track 6   Autoharp, Mic 1, AT 4050 12" in front. (Bryan Bowers, Voyager Recording)

Autoharp, Mic 2, AT4050 12" in front, blended with Mic 2, Sony ECM50 lavaliere pinned to chest.

Track 7   Banjo, Mic 1, AKG C3000,12" pointed at center of head. (Harley Bray, Voyager Recording)

Banjo, Mic 2, AKG C3000, 12" in front of head, just inside rim at end of fingerboard.

Banjo, Mic 3, AKG C3000, 6" in front, pointing 3" inside head 1/2 way between bridge and rim.

Banjo, Mic 4, AKG C3000, 2' in front of player's head, pointed down toward middle of head.

Track 8   Bass, acoustic, Mic 1, AKG C3000, 6" above "sweet spot" on treble bout, away from player (Ron Holdridge, Voyager Recording)

Bass, acoustic, Mic 2, AKG C3000 4" out from center of f hole away from player, blended with Mic 1.

Track 9   Bass, electric, Mic 1, Shure SM57 2" out from outer edge of cone.

Track 10   Bassoon, Mic 1, AKG C3000, 2' away at middle of keys. (Melony Hertel, Shoreline Community College)

Bassoon, Mic 2, AKG C3000 near bell.

Track 11   Bodhran, AKG C3000 18" in front of rim away from player. (Ed Hartman, The Drum Exchange)

Track 12   Cello, Mic 1, AKG C3000 6" in front of bridge. (Mike Matesky)

Cello, Mic 2, AKG C3000 16" in front of bridge.

Track 13   Clarinet, Mic 1, AKG C1000S, aimed at lower finger holes 1' away. (Doug Reed, Shoreline Community College)

Clarinet, Mic 2, AKG C1000S, 2" from bell, pointed at rim of bell.

Track 14   Dobro, Mic 1, AKG C1000 12" above

treble sound hole away from performer, pointed at soundhole. (Orville Johnson, Voyager Recording)

Dobro, Mic 2, AKG C1000 6" above bridge, pointed at bridge.

Dobro, Mic 3, AKG C1000 6" above tailpiece, pointed down at top.

Dobro, Mic Setup 4, AKG C1000 6" in front of front edge, 2" above front edge, pointed across the top between the bridge and end of fingerboard.

Track 15   Kick drum, Mic 1, rear head off, inside drum, 2" off front head, centered, AKG D112. (Michael Cotta, Robert Lang Recording)

Kick Drum, Mic 2, rear head off, inside drum off center, 2" from head, AKG D112.

Kick drum, Mic 3, rear head off, inside drum, on center, 12" from head, AKG D112.

Kick drum, Mic 4, rear head on, mic centered on head, 2" off head, AKG D112.

Kick drum, Mic 5, rear head on, mic off-center, 2" off head, AKG D112.

Track 16   Snare drum, Mic 1, 1" above head, just inside top rim, Shure SM57.

Snare drum, Mic 2, 2" off bottom, just inside rim, AKG 414, phase reversed, mixed with Mic 1, Shure SM58, above top head.

Snare drum, Mic 3, lapel mic suspended 1' up from head and 1" inside rim, AKG C567.

Track 17　Hi-hat, Mic 1, 3" above edge, AKG 414.

Hi-hat, Mic 2, equal distance between hi-hat and snare to pick up both, bidirectional, AKG 414.

Track 18　High toms, Mic 1, 1" above head and 2" inside rim, Sennheiser 421.

High toms, Mic 2, single mic between both high toms, Sennheiser 421.

Track 19　Low toms, 3" above head, 2" inside rim, AKG C3000.

Track 20　Cymbals, Mic 1, cardioid condenser mics 6" above the rim of each cymbal, on the side away from the player, Calrec 2050s.

Cymbals, Mic 2, stereo pair 2' above and spaced over the respective left and right cymbal groups, Calrec 2050 cardioids.

Cymbals, Mic 3, stereo pair, overhead spaced 3:1, Calrec 2050s.

Cymbals, Stereo Mic 4, X-Y coincident pair, 3' above, centered, Calrec 2050s.

Track 21　Drums, minimal miking.

Track 22　Hand drum (Dumbek), Mic 1, 8" in front of head and to side, Neumann TLM170. (Dave Huber, Robert Lang Recording)

Hand drum (Dumbek), Mic 2, Calrec 2050 omni 8" off rear port, Neumann TLM170 8" off the head, off center, blended to stereo, phase reversed on rear mic.

Hand drum (Dumbek), Mic 3, Neumann TLM 170, 8' from drummer, 5' off floor.

Track 23　Flute, transverse, Mic 1, AKG C1000S, pointed at player's left hand position from 12" away. (Doug Reed, Shoreline Community College)

Flute, transverse, Mic 2, AKG C1000S, 5' away from player at height of top of player's head, pointed at instrument.

Flute, transverse, Mic 3, AKG C1000S, 4" above mouthpiece pointed down.

Track 24　Guitar, acoustic, Mic 1, AKG C1000 12" above end of fingerboard. (Orville Johnson, Voyager Recordings)

Guitar, acoustic, Mic 2, AKG C1000 12" above bridge, nylon strung guitar.

Guitar, acoustic, Mic 3, AT4050 "Rising sun."

Guitar, acoustic, Mic 4, AKG C1000 5" above sound hole, pointed at end of fingerboard.

Guitar, acoustic, Mic 5, AT4050 2" behind bridge, even with first string, 4" up from top.

Guitar, acoustic, Mic Setup 6— Mic 1, AT4050, 12" above end of fingerboard, blended with Mic 6, AKG C1000, pointed at back of guitar from 3" out, 5" in from end of instrument, out of phase.

Guitar, acoustic, Mic Setup 7— Mic 1, AT4050, 12" over end of fingerboard, and Mic 5, AKG C1000, 2" behind bridge and 4" above top, in spaced stereo.

Track 25   Guitar, electric, Mic 1, 12" in front of center of speaker, Shure SM57, (Joe Vinikow, Voyager Recording)

Guitar, electric, Mic 2, 2" in front of center of speaker, Shure SM57.

Guitar, electric Mic 3, 4" in front of edge of speaker cone, Shure SM57.

Guitar, electric, Mic Setup 4— Mic 3, Shure SM57, 4" in front of edge of speaker cone; Mic 4, AKG 414, 6' in front of speaker; mics blended to mono.

Guitar, electric, Mic Setup 5— Mic 3, Shure SM57, 4" in front of edge of speaker cone in front; Mic 5, AKG 414, 6" from back, center of speaker, out of phase; mics blended.

Track 26   Harp, Irish, Mic 1, AKG C3000, 6" off sound board at about middle. (John Peekstok, Dusty Strings)

Harp, Mic 2, AKG C3000, 2' back from instrument at about height of player's head, pointed at center of sound board.

Track 27   Mandolin (Neapolitan), Mic 1, Audio-Technica 4050 18" in front of sound hole. (Phil Williams, Voyager Recording)

Mandolin, Gibson F-5, Mic 2, Audio-Technica 4050, 18" in front of lower f-hole.

Track 28   Organ, Pipe Mic Setup 1, coincident stereo, AKGC3000s (Rick Paulsen, First Church of Christ Scientist, Renton, WA)

Organ, Pipe Mic Setup 2, Spaced stereo AKG C3000s

Organ, Pipe, Mic Setup 3, Spaced

Pair, Radio Shack (Modified) PZMs

Track 29   Congas, Mics 1, AKG C3000s 3" above head, 2" in from rim. (Ed Hartman, The Drum Exchange)

Congas, Mics 2, AKG C3000s 12" above head, 2" in from rim.

Track 30   Piano, Grand, Mic 1, PZM on lid. (Terry Wergeland, Robert Lang Recording)

Piano, Grand, Mic Setup 2, spaced pair, 6" above strings, one above high and one above low strings, Calrec 2050 cardioids.

Piano, Grand, Mic Setup 3, coincident pair 12" inside rim and 12" above strings, Calrec 2050 cardioids.

Piano, Grand, Mic Setup 4, Coincident pair just outside rim facing into lid, 18" higher than strings, Calrec 2050 cardioids.

Piano, Grand, Mic Setup 5, Spaced stereo pair just outside rim, 18" higher than strings, Calrec 2050 cardioids.

Piano, Grand, Mic Setup 6, Spaced stereo pair 2' apart and 5" over hammers, Calrec 2050 cardioids.

Track 31   Piano, Upright, Mic Setup 1, AKG C3000 over top (Vivian Williams, Voyager Recording)

Piano, Upright, Mic Setup 2, AKG C3000 8" off treble & bass strings, front removed

Piano, upright, Mic 3, AKG C3000 coincident stereo over player's head

Piano, upright Mic Setup 4, AKG C3000 treble & bass in kickboard area

Piano, upright, Mic Setup 5, PZMs behind

Track 32   Saxophone, Mic 1, AKG C1000S, 1' away from instrument, pointed 3" above top of bell. (Doug Reed, Shoreline Community College)

Saxophone, Mic 2, AKG C1000S, 3" from bell, off-center, aimed at edge of bell.

Track 33   Tympani, Mic 1, AKG C3000S, 2' over left and right drum. (Dave Huber, Shoreline Community College)

Track 34   Trombone, Mic 1, Neumann TLM170, cardioid, 10 dB pad, 6" in front of bell and to the side. (Barry Ehrlich, Shoreline Community College)

Track 35   Trumpet, Mic 1, Neumann TLM170 condenser mic, 12" in front of bell and to side. (Brad Hendry. Shoreline Community College)

Trumpet, Mic 2, Shure SM57 dynamic mic, 12" in front of bell and to side.

Trumpet , Mic 3, RCA 44BX ribbon mic, 12" in front of bell and to side.

Track 36   Violin, Mic 1, 18" in front of player at just above forehead level, pointed at chin, Neumann TLM170 in cardioid. (Sande Gillette, Robert Lang Recording)

Violin, Mic 2, 5' in front of player, 8' off floor, pointed at violin, Neumann TLM170 in cardioid.

Violin, Mic 3, 8" above strings, just behind bridge, pointed at strings, Neumann TLM170 in cardioid.

Track 37   Fiddle, Mic 1, AT4050, 18" in front of player at level of player's forehead, pointed at the player's chin. (Vivian Williams, Voyager Recording)

Fiddle, Mic 2, AT4050, 18" in front of player at level of player's forehead, pointed at the player's chin; Mic 4, AKG C1000, pointed at center of back of fiddle, 6" out; mics

Index

Symbols